# The Grouse Hunter's Almanac

# The
# Grouse Hunter's
# Almanac

## Chris Dorsey
### Foreword by David Wonderlich

Voyageur Press

To Leo and Ruby Dorsey, for years of tolerating
my bird dogs, bird pens, and birdbrain ideas

Text copyright © 1990 by Chris Dorsey
Foreword copyright © 1990 by David Wonderlich
Photography copyrights as noted by each photograph

Illustrations on pages 74 and 76 by Renee Graef, from "A Grouse in Hand," produced by the Depar
ment of Agricultural Journalism, University of Wisconsin–Madison, courtesy of Scott R. Craven, co-
author.

Printed in the United States of America
First hardcover edition
90  91  92  93  94  5  4  3  2  1
First softcover edition
99  00  01  02  03  6  5  4  3  2

**Library of Congress Cataloging-in-Publication Data**

Dorsey, Chris, 1965–
        The grouse hunter's almanac / Chris Dorsey ; foreword by David Wonderlich
        Includes bibiliographical references and index.
    ISBN 0-89658-135-7
    ISBN 0-89658-261-2 (pbk.)
    1. Ruffed grouse shooting. 2. Ruffed grouse. I. Title.
    SK325.G7D67   1990
    799.2'48616—dc20                              90-43400
                                                    CIP

Published by Voyageur Press, Inc.
123 North Second Street
P.O. Box 338
Stillwater, MN 55082 U.S.A.
651-430-2210, fax 651-430-2211


Distributed in Canada by Raincoast Books
8680 Cambie Street
Vancouver, B.C. V6P 6M9

Voyageur Press books are also available at discounts for quantities for educational, fundraising, premium,
or sales-promotion use. For details contact the marketing department. Please write or call for our free
catalog of natural history publications.

# Contents

# Acknowledgments

This book was made possible through the cooperation and assistance of many people—what follows is only a partial list of those who contributed. My gratitude goes first to five beloved gun dog writers who shared their understanding of the relationship between dog and grouse as only they could: Charley Dickey, Dave Duffey, Johnny Falk, Bill Tarrant, and Charley Waterman. They are gentlemen all. My special thanks and well wishes go to David Wonderlich, a fine writer and editor. I am indebted to my favorite hunting partners and good friends Gary Wilson, Phil Brodbeck, Chuck Petrie, Steve Ballentine, and Keith Gilbertson who all, at one time or another, sacrificed hunting time so that I might take photographs.

My thanks go also to Herb Lange, Dave Otto, Tom Martinson, Dan Small, Bob Robb, Dave Fletcher, David Kenyon, Mary Block, Dave Hetzler, and David Hall, whose outstanding photographs were integral in creating this book. To biologists John Kubisiak, Don Rusch, Gordon Gullion, Sue Marcquenski, Ron Burkert, and Scott Craven, I owe much for their technical support and research wizardry.

Others making this book possible are George and Kay Evans, honorary President and First Lady of American grouse hunting. Ken Szabo's dandy newsletter, *Grouse Tales*, proved a valuable source of information for this book, too. Likewise, Doug Truax, Tim Joseph, and Fred Lawson were also instrumental in this project's development.

The following authors have all made contributions to this book and to the best of American sporting literature: Tom Anderson, Stephen Bodio, Dave Carty, Gene Hill, Robert Jones, Ron Rau, Nick Sisley, Steve Smith, Dennis Walrod, and Frank Woolner.

This acknowledgment would not be complete if I failed to thank my sister-in-law, Kathy Fitch Dorsey, for her long-distance computer consulting. She rescued me from the depths of computer depression on several occasions.

Lastly, my sanity is intact because of the most understanding woman I know, Lori Phillips, who tolerated my preoccupation with this project and even encouraged it.

# Foreword

Editors of hunting magazines have a continuous flow of manuscripts cross their desks. Out of this flow from time to time one writer's work stands out from all the rest; it has a special quality that brings the reader in contact with more than each individual fact or anecdote; it transports us beyond our armchair to the coverts—we can hear the tingle of our setter's bell, smell the damp earth, feel the cold metal of our double cradled in expectancy, and taste the excitement of a grouse's explosive rise. Chris Dorsey is one of those rare writers who elicits these feelings, and he brings the spirit of hunts past and the dream of future days afield to the present.

Chris's background is well-established in the publishing industry. He is the past editor of Wisconsin, Minnesota, and Michigan Sportsman magazines and is currently feature editor with Petersen's *Hunting* magazine. He has written for a variety of magazines on the subjects of grouse and grouse hunting: *Shooting Sportsman, Field & Stream, Sports Afield, Hunting,* and many more. Even in his earlier years his love of the upland covert was already developed with college English papers including such works as "Playing Hooky with Grouse," "Partridge Days and Partridge Nights," "Confessions of a Grouse," and "If I Were a Grouse." Chris's roots are in rural Wisconsin where he developed his affection for setters and grouse. Since then, he has spent countless hours wandering through grouse coverts, musing about the mysteries of ruffed grouse.

He is a hunter who once drove a thousand miles in a weekend to hunt woodcock in Mississippi. His setter produced a single point on woodcock. He missed. Despite his failure to bag even one bird, Dorsey's passion for grouse and woodcock have caused him to travel across the continent from Georgia to Alberta in search of one or both of these birds.

Dorsey calls ruffed grouse hunting "the most compelling, challenging, and damn maddening sport in America." And he can't resist the allure of it all. He spends most of October, November, and parts of December with those who feel the same way. "Grouse," he says, "are the alibi every hunter needs to escape those who don't understand upland bird hunting." Chris also thinks every grouse hunter should digest a little Aldo Leopold, as they would their daily dose of fiber. I believe if one could read a little Chris Dorsey a day, the hunter's world would always be closer at hand, and with the turn of a page, grouse and woodcock seasons would never be too far off.

DAVID WONDERLICH, EDITOR
*SHOOTING SPORTSMAN*

*There are two kinds of hunting: ordinary hunting and ruffed-grouse hunting.*
—Aldo Leopold, *A Sand County Almanac*

# Introduction
# The Allegory of the Covert

A sk me why I hunt grouse, and I'll ask you why you breathe.

Sometimes I wonder if grouse aren't hunting me. I sit in an office high-rise surrounded by auto-choked streets. Inside my cubical I muse, recalling my young setter's first water retrieve or a wily grouse's evasion of my wrath on four consecutive occasions. The walls of my office are a memorial to past hunts as portraits remind me of splendid days with grouse, dogs, and friends.

It is often a bittersweet experience, though, to look at the memories. Each photo is inviting, yet I am reminded that my oldest setter—still a pup in one snapshot—will likely not make another full season. There are the friends whom I haven't seen in years and the coverts that I wish were still the same, yet know have long since become farm fields or development fodder. But always, undiscovered coverts await exploration; that thought comes to haunt me each October.

Perhaps I hunt grouse because I am gauging myself. Maybe I know that all will be right in my universe if I am able to locate a grouse, flush it, and, of course, miss it. Such a hunt will recreate the one event that has stayed constant in my life, a life otherwise filled with inexorable change.

When love has failed, the workplace is a wreck, and my finances are a shambles, I always know that there are grouse to chase—and the rest of the world be damned while I'm in a covert. Perhaps I hunt grouse because it is something I am good at. It's not that I kill many grouse, but I let the hunt consume me. I can forget almost anything while afield. It is important for a grouse hunter to concentrate on nothing when hunting grouse, for a good grouse hunter, like a fine writer, must have a clear mind and let the grouse, like the muse, flavor his thoughts. How, may

I ask, can you be ready for the split-second chance at a grouse when your brain is cluttered with thoughts of loan papers, bills, or work deadlines?

Something subliminal absorbs grouse hunters when they enter the cathedral of a covert. Grouse hunting can be a renewal for those who let the healing powers of the covert work its magic. I used to think the orchard covert was something of an Eden. My old, arthritic setter becomes a pup the moment he passes the windmill and scents the descendants of grouse he chased a decade ago. I smile in wonderment, thinking that perhaps this is our first world, our fountain of youth. When, alas, there is no more light in his eyes, I shall make a pilgrimage to the orchard and bury him where I know there will always be grouse for him to chase. Perhaps, someday, when my knees no longer bend the way they once did and my eyes cannot focus clearly, I will hear the ringing of his bell in the orchard one more time. Then, if only for a moment, maybe the pain will go from my knees and I will once again see the world as I did when I chased grouse with him from the apple trees.

Grouse hunting has always brought me closest to the people that mean the most to me. They are my friends not because they hunt grouse; they are my friends because they share the same view of grouse. This is an epiphany that comes into clear focus each time I stare into a campfire, surrounded by hunters who see the same things in the dancing flames. Perhaps grouse coverts are the alibi each of us needs to get away from people who will never see the virtue of following a dog through the aspens. There are, after all, friends—and there are grouse-hunting friends. A friend understands that I must hunt, but a grouse-hunting friend knows why I hunt.

I am so afflicted with a passion for the coverts that I can scarcely drive through good grouse country without daydreaming of pointing dogs and flushing grouse. It is an ailment particularly acute in September, but almost critical by October. Fortunately, it's nothing that a dose of No. 8 shot and a setter won't cure in a couple of weeks in the aspen—or perhaps a month or two.

Next year, when the aspen turn yellow, the tamarack to gold, and the sumac to crimson, my friends and I will once again find in our lives sanity where once there was confusion. We will rediscover purpose in place of misdirection and rekindle spirit where fire had dwindled.

# A Year in the Life

*Though land use is harmful to other game birds, our grouse will continue to beat his drums in springtime and confound gunners in November. He will do this because his stamping ground is now, and always has been, the rough, rugged country that is last delivered up to the plow and bulldozer.*

—Frank Woolner, *Grouse and Grouse Hunting*

# A Year in the Life

Though I've yet to discover the journal entries by the inaugural European travelers in North America that describe their first encounters with ruffed grouse, I can imagine the adventure. Initial reports to Europe must have told of a bird that could defoliate an entire tree with thunder. Sketches depicted a winged whirlwind fit for a medieval bestiary. A log entry breathlessly noted "the birds flush with such fury they seem to leave in their wake a vacuum in time." It was another way of saying the flush of a grouse very likely scared the bejesus out of these intrepid explorers.

I felt much the same way upon my first encounter with a ruffed grouse. I'm not sure I actually saw the bird, but my electrified nerves told me that the momentary tornado before me was, indeed, a ruffed grouse.

Several years passed before I actually held a grouse in hand. It wound up in my grip not because I shot the bird, but because I happened by a hunter who did.

With a keen eye, I examined that grouse. The first bit of anatomy to catch my attention was the bird's protruding neck ruff, a collar of dark, iridescent feathers that gives the ruffed grouse its common name. In size, the grouse fell midway between a pheasant and a Hungarian partridge, seventeen or eighteen inches from beak to tail tip. Its slim body must have weighed about a pound and a half, the average for the species. The back feathers of the bird were a uniform mottled russet, perfectly woven to the base of the tail. In time, over many hunts in many coverts of North America, I would see grouse in plumages that vary in subtle gradients of color from red to brown to gray. And I would learn that the hens are slightly smaller, a little more quietly colored, and more delicately ruffed and tail-feathered than their male counterparts.

The handsome tail fan of a ruff is to a grouse hunter what a set of antlers is to a deer hunter. The bird I held was a male, and his trophy tail was exceptionally long, with a thick brown band framing the tip of tail feathers.

This cock was dressed for winter; feathering extended down the legs, all the way to the base of the feet. On his feet appeared another adaptation to life in wintry regions. Tiny scales, called pectinations, sprouted along his toes. Most likely, these scales assist grouse to grip icy tree branches while the birds feed on buds and seeds.

We spread the drummer's wings; they spanned roughly twenty-three inches. I folded them and held silence and thunder.

In order for there to be grouse (*Bonasa umbellus*), there must, of course, be grouse habitat. In much of the bird's range, aspen is to grouse what corn is to pheasant. The difference is that grouse favor a mixture of different age-classes of aspen in order not only to survive, but to thrive.

While intensive agribusiness has caused the decline of many farmland wildlife species like pheasant and quail, ruffed grouse benefit immeasurably by human disturbance of the forest. Before the use of poplar for pulp, grouse were dependent upon forest fires to spark woodland regeneration. An insatiable need for paper and paper products has led to continual cropping of many forests in the Great Lakes and New England regions.

While clear-cutting aspen is an important way to gain the kind of stand regeneration necessary to benefit grouse and scores of other forest species, clear-cuts encompassing large tracts of land are a detriment to the cause of most wildlife—including grouse. A simple formula I was taught in a college wildlife management course used a forty-acre woodlot for an example. Dr. Lyle Nauman, my advisor and instructor for the course, drew a square representing the forty-acre woods. He then divided the square into four equal parts, each sector representing ten acres. He advocated cutting one of the ten-acre sections every ten years. This forty-year rotation provided grouse with several different age-classes of regenerating aspen. It was a simple formula that remains valid even today.

It is also important to understand exactly why grouse need this diversity to thrive. And in areas where aspen isn't present, how are grouse able to survive? Discover some of the answers in this look at the seasons of the grouse.

## SPRING

To the unlearned, the sound of a distant grouse drumming is just another unexplained noise of the forest. I sometimes think that I fly-fish not to catch fish, but to survey my favorite coverts through the sounds of these peculiar drummings. I ponder between casts, How have the grouse fared the winter? Drummers seem to celebrate their survival with the whirring crescendo of wing beats. Ironically, it is this same phenomenon that gets many of them killed at the hands—or, in this season, the talons—of predators.

A male grouse concentrates its drumming on what biologists call a primary log. This "log" may indeed be a log, or the drumming site may be any number of suitable platforms, including boulders, wood piles, tree roots, and rock walls. It's within roughly five acres of this log that drummers spend much of their late winter and early spring. In northern climes, snow may still be on the ground when drumming can be heard in the woods. A male commonly selects a log the previous fall and may, in fact, have defended it from other grouse throughout the winter. An Ontario study revealed that 96 percent of male grouse stayed within 164 feet of their primary drumming log during the winter months.

As the forest warms in spring, the drummer returns to his station and actively seeks to seduce a receptive hen to his log. An ideal drumming trunk gives him an elevated vantage from which to spot both hens and intruders. Equally critical is a protective shelter of woody cover overhead, to allow him time to escape an attack from above—namely by goshawks and owls.

When a hen is ready, she will approach the drummer for mating, which only lasts a few seconds. The hen then scurries forth to begin constructing a makeshift nest. A grouse nest will never leave anyone impressed by the engineering abilities of its maker. It is little more than a small depression in the leaves— it is, nonetheless, all that is required. Quite often, a nest is found adjacent to a stone or beneath a fallen tree, as if the hen prefers protection from at least one attack route. According to some studies, grouse seem particularly fond of nesting in hardwoods where there is little obstruction at ground level. Like the drummer, however, the hen requires protection from above. The open floor allows her ample opportunity to spot approaching ground predators, at which time she commonly leaves the nest in an attempt to lure them away by pretending she is injured. Once the threat has passed, the hen returns to the nest to continue the incubation process. The male, meanwhile, continues his performances in an attempt to lure other females to his log. His efforts persist until late spring, a time when most hens are tending to chicks or are resting atop a clutch of eggs.

Once all the eggs in the clutch have been laid, the hen begins to incubate them and spends almost the entire day setting on them. Producing the eggs is a physical-

Grouse-hunting friends. (*Photo © by Chris Dorsey*)

Southern grouse habitat is far different from the aspen-alder forests of many of the northern states. Mountain laurel, hemlock, and rhododendron are three plant species associated with southern birds. (*Photo © by Chris Dorsey*)

Every grouse seems to have its thorn. But grouse utilize a wide variety of plant species in their extensive range. (*Photo © by Chris Dorsey*)

Within a couple of weeks of hatching, grouse chicks are able to make short-leap flights to low tree branches where they can elude many predators. (*Photo © by Tom Martinson*)

By grazing woodlands, farmers are preventing the growth of an understory—a critical component in any productive grouse and woodcock habitat. (*Photo © by Chris Dorsey*)

Drumming logs are essential stages for males to advertise their availability to females. The best logs are surrounded by a forest understory that protects drummers from avian predators. (*Photo courtesy of the Wisconsin DNR*)

Shortly after a grouse reaches four months of age, it embarks on a journey to new cover. This dispersal ensures the health and survival of the species. (*Photo © by John Kubisiak*)

Goshawks and owls like this are the chief predators of wintering grouse. The better the grouse habitat, the lower the chances of raptors successfully snatching grouse. (*Photo © by Tom Martinson*)

Grouse hens commonly construct their nests on open forest floor. Such sites allow hens to see approaching predators. (*Photo © by John Kubisiak*)

Grouse authority Gordon Gullion of Minnesota believes that plants such as aspen may—from time to time—produce chemicals in their buds that are toxic to grouse. These poisonous phenolic compounds may weaken grouse or force them to seek other, less nutritious forms of food. (*Photo © by Tom Martinson*)

These newly hatched chicks face a variety of threats enroute to adulthood. Predation, weather, and disease claim up to half of them before they reach their tenth week—despite the diligent protection of the hen. (*Photo © by Herb Lange*)

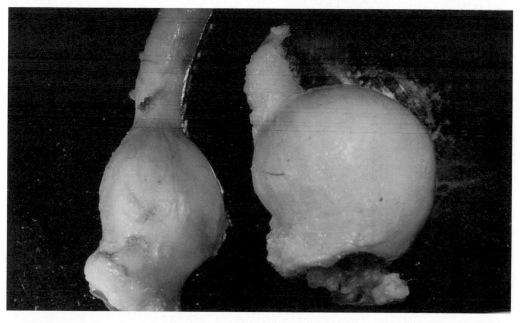

The grouse stomach at left was taken from a healthy bird. The stomach at right was infected with the dispharynx roundworm. The parasite causes blockage in the stomach, thus weakening the grouse to the point that it becomes more susceptible to disease and predation. (*Photo © by Mary Block*)

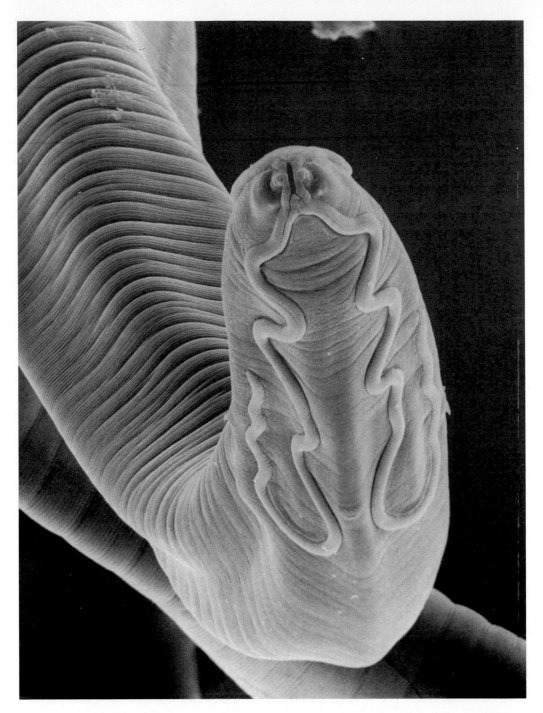

This roundworm, *Dispharynx nasuta*, has been implicated in the cyclic swings of ruffed grouse populations throughout the Great Lakes states. Though it is still uncertain just how much impact the parasite has on overall grouse populations, research continues into its effects on the birds. (*Photo © by Mary Block*)

This immature great horned owl will soon join the ranks of its parents and goshawks in becoming an efficient predator in the uplands. Grouse suffer their heaviest losses to avian predators during the winter months. The better the grouse habitat, the lower the chances raptors have to successfully snatch grouse. (*Photo © by Tom Martinson*)

Vermont hunters, Doug Truax (*left*) and Tim Joseph, work thick forest edges that grouse so often favor. During the early season when foliage typically prevents clear shooting, one hunter may find luck by hunting the outside edge of cover. (*Photo © by Chris Dorsey*)

When the population of snowshoe hares is at a low level in Canada, avian predators like hawks and owls often fly south in search of food. These birds prey heavily on grouse in the northern tier of states. It's believed that this phenomenon may be an integral part of the grouse cycle. (*Photo © by Tom Martinson*)

Shortly after the chicks hatch, the hen will lead her brood to heavy cover where they begin dining on insects. (*Photo © by Tom Martinson*)

Grouse hunting gave rise to the term "snap shooting." While these hunters know their chances of hitting a grouse flushing in this thicket are low, they improve their odds by holding their gun stocks just under the armpit, thus reducing the time that it takes to mount and fire. (*Photo © by Chris Dorsey*)

Recognizing prime grouse habitat does not always require on-site inspection. By cross-referencing a topographic map, plat book, and aerial photographs, hunters can identify likely ruffed grouse cover as well as the person who owns the land. (*Photo © by Bob Robb*)

Although grouse may travel several miles during fall dispersal, almost all the travel is done on foot. (*Photo © by John Kubisiak*)

ly taxing proposition for the hen, so it is important that food be located nearby to allow her to replenish her nutrient loss. It remains important during incubation, too, because she will only leave the nest for brief periods of feeding in the morning and evening. The quality of her protein intake during egg laying has a direct bearing on the health and survival of the developing chicks.

According to grouse biologists, hens typically feed within one hundred yards of the nest. At this season of the year, the hen often can choose to eat from a variety of plants, but she commonly selects young leaves in the low branches of nearby immature aspen, hawthorn, witch hazel, or other desirable species.

Once the chicks hatch, they mature at an incredible rate. Within hours they are dry and standing. Despite the fact that the eggs might have been laid gradually for two weeks, they hatch nearly in unison. That is a handy adaptation because the hen is anxious to move the chicks to a new location. Within a week, the chicks' primary feathers are nearly developed, and they are beginning to try their luck at short flights. Their newfound ability not only helps them elude predators, but assists them in catching insects, an important source of sustenance during the early weeks of development.

Hen and chicks live in areas with a relatively open forest floor. The chicks are scarcely larger than a bumble bee, so heavy brush can be nearly impenetrable for the tiny birds. The edges of forest openings become important for chicks because they provide suitable protection from predators and because where thick vegetation and sunshine meet insects are found in higher concentrations. Ferns also offer protection for the chicks while allowing them to move freely on the floor of the woods.

In years with extremely dry weather, insect production is reduced and so are the chances for the chicks' survival. Berry bushes, shrubs, and saplings are commonly found along forest openings and are most likely to provide an optimal environment for the chicks during dry or wet springs. The hen serves as both protector and shelter for the chicks during bad weather. Despite her diligent guardianship, however, upwards of half of the chicks will be lost by their tenth week. If they endure until their fifth or sixth week, chicks begin sampling plant parts such as flowers, buds, and leaves.

## SUMMER
With the onset of summer, the chicks have begun using the habitat that will serve them for much of their adult life. In areas where aspen is the predominant forest

species, stands from six to twenty-six years in age have shown to be most suitable for grouse. Alder, hazel, dogwood, poison sumac, willow, and birch are a few other species known to be attractive to ruffed grouse. With such an extensive range, however, it is impossible to catalog here all the species used by grouse, but the bird has proven adaptable to many different environs.

I recall how utterly lost I felt on my first Appalachian grouse hunt. The aspen of my Yankee forest was replaced with the laurel of Dixie—a species looking odd to me, as though it belonged in an Amazonian forest. Small drainages choked with laurel and holly—two words sounding remarkably close to Laurel and Hardy given the appropriate degree of Southern accent—proved to be the Confederate version of aspen and alder. These two species housed virtually every grouse I flushed below the Mason-Dixon Line.

Whether searching for southern, western, or northern ruffed grouse, however, it is difficult—with any certainty—to pinpoint where a ruff might reside in the summer months. During this season a grouse has a plethora of suitable cover types available to it. Many of these habitats may be unsuitable to the birds earlier or later in the year when dense leaves aren't present. The thick vegetation of summer offers grouse increased protection from predation, especially as birds also undergo a molt. While they never enter a true flightless period, many birds—both chicks and adults—choose to run from threats during this phase. Because of this defensive behavior they become vulnerable for a short period during the molt. Imagine being able to fly through a war zone one day, the next morning having to walk the same course. It's little wonder grouse seem to develop an identifiable neurosis by hunting season and flush wildly—sometimes through kitchen windows and the like.

## FALL

I suspect grouse harbor as much anticipation about fall as many hunters do—only for very different reasons. While hunters wax romantic about their favorite coverts, grouse are faced with an increasing number of life-and-death decisions. Where leaves once filled the firmament providing a protective cloak overhead, now barren branches serve as ideal perches from which raptors can survey the surrounding forest floor. Further complicating a grouse's life is a gradual decline of available food. If that weren't enough, days grow shorter and the temperature drops, thus adding to a cumulative deterioration of life for the grouse.

The bountiful summer months seem little more than a fattening period for ruffs and other wildlife before nature's harvest gets underway in earnest. Each species—

including the human—plays out its role as predator or prey in a drama that has evolved for millennia. It is a repetitious game in which I sometimes wonder if I am not just a very small pawn, a Lilliputian of sorts, who sees only the minute world around me while someone or something understands why life and death share the same continuum.

It is fall, I think, of all the seasons that illuminates these thoughts so vividly for me. While the seasonal adjustments in my life are little more than a simple matter of storm windows and snow tires, dynamic changes are underway in the grouse woods. The individual grouse's urge to break from the family flock intensifies as the need to find a covert of its own grows with summer's coming to a close. A male grouse typically disperses until he finds an unoccupied drumming log of his own. Occasionally a hunter will flush grouse from unlikely cover. Generally, these ruffs are juvenile birds seeking to find their own space in life. The odds of surviving a winter in marginal habitat are stacked significantly against the grouse—though a bird that has made it this far in development has already defied most odds. Females are known to disperse far greater distances than their male counterparts, leading some to believe that they suffer a higher mortality rate during dispersal than do the males. It is not uncommon for hens to travel eight to ten miles during dispersal—short flights are intermixed with a surprising amount of walking during this period.

## WINTER

Although ruffed grouse are as well suited to cold and snow as virtually any bird save ptarmigan, winter can be especially brutal—even for grouse. Unlike other galliformes, grouse are not negatively impacted by heavy snow. To the contrary, deep snow is quite often a blessing for grouse. While other birds such as pheasant and quail must scratch to find their food buried under snow, grouse look upon the powder as a welcome source of insulation from bitter temperatures. When a grouse is finished feeding on mature poplar catkins, it merely dives headlong into the snow and roosts for the night. The submerged grouse tunnels into a comfort zone where it may sit for a few minutes or for days. One study indicated that snow roosts allow grouse to conserve 30 percent more energy than if they were exposed directly to the elements.

A walk through a winter woodlot in the North is a stark reminder of the struggle wildlife faces with plummeting temperatures and heavy snow. There are no longer any leaves to shield grouse from wind, an especially mortal enemy when matched with snow and sleet. Where once there was food aplenty, a meal can become a scarce commodity. It is in the dead of winter that the appeal of migration takes on heightened appeal to humans and, I suspect, would to snowbound grouse if they knew of such possibilities.

As much as powdery snow can be a benefit to grouse, however, snow encrusted with a layer of ice can be lethal to grouse. The birds sometimes unwittingly plunge into the ice expecting a soft entry. Instead, the impact on the ice may break a wing or injure the grouse, leaving it unable to survive the gauntlet of predators that may inhabit the area. Common January thaws and freezes can sometimes be a catastrophe for grouse for this reason. Birds may also become trapped beneath a layer of ice as the snow melts during a warm afternoon and freezes again during the night.

Research suggests that grouse need roughly ten inches of powdery snow in which to make their tunnels. If there is less snow on the ground, however, they will still nestle into it for added protection against thermal loss. In areas of the grouse range where snow is either uncommon or found in insufficient quantities to be of value to grouse, the birds often utilize conifers or similar dense vegetation as a way to reduce heat loss. There is also speculation by some biologists that these same conifers can be something of a trap for grouse as avian predators use the same cover. Nevertheless, pines and spruce can significantly reduce wind, thereby allowing grouse to further conserve their body heat.

It is a complete grouse hunter who understands not only how to kill his quarry, but the grand scheme of events that created and sustained the life taken in a fleeting moment. As I stare at a freshly killed grouse resting in my palm, I cannot help but pay tribute to the bird—even if it is merely a silent pause in an otherwise hurried journey through the aspens.

# The Mysterious Cycle

*I suspect that for as long as ruffed grouse live in our northern regions, they will appear to be moving towards extinction about every 10 years, but become moderately to truly plentiful four or five years later.*

*—Gordon Gullion, Grouse of the North Shore*

# The Mysterious Cycle

The ruffed grouse cycle, or "the cycle" as it is known to most grouse hunters, is a phenomenon around which serious hunters plan their lives. In the northern parts of ruffed grouse range, the bird's numbers tend to vary periodically. The populations fluctuate with such regularity and significance that these changes are termed "cycles." One acquaintance quit his high-salaried position in Atlanta to return to the forests of northern Minnesota where he grew up chasing ruffs from the aspen forests. Reports of a grouse flock reaching the pinnacle of its ten-year cycle were enough to prompt his return to the North.

The cycle is an event, something hunters plan litters of bird-dog pups around. Conventional wisdom among grouse hunters suggests that it is always best to start a pup when grouse populations are high. The logic, of course, is that the pupil will learn the way of the grouse at an impressionable age and when there is an abundance of ruffs. Moreover, when the cycle tailspins, the owner should have had time to rid the youngster of puppyhood quirks, and by now Pup should have become a skilled companion in the forest—one capable of uncovering grouse during the grimmest of years.

Unjustly, and sadly, grouse dogs seldom see more than one complete cycle. The death of a good dog is a solemn and sobering experience because a companion dies and because that death reminds us of our own mortality. I wonder, Why must it end so?—and toss another shovel of earth backward through time while a grave of sorts is completed in my soul, each particle of soil representing moments spent in years past. The cycle encompasses the gradual preparation a person undergoes knowing that a very dear life is to end. Perhaps there is something fitting, though, about grouse populations and grouse dogs sharing the same cycle of life.

## VARIRATIONS IN FOOD QUALITY

The grouse cycle is more prevalent in the northern half of the bird's range. Several theories—some more plausible than others—seek to explain what causes this unique phenomenon. One of the more intriguing ones is Gordon Gullion's idea that plants—like aspen—from time to time produce chemicals in their buds that may be toxic to grouse. Gullion, a biologist and ruffed grouse expert, believes that aspen trees may be able to crudely communicate to each other since they are clones interconnected by a vast system of rhizomes. It's thought that the plants are able to do so by relaying these phenolic compounds through the rhizomes.

The phenols and tannins make the aspen buds less palatable to grouse, thereby forcing them to seek other forms of sustenance. Often, these alternative foods are less nutritious and more difficult to find. In the process of locating another food source, grouse may become weakened and susceptible to maladies and predators. Self-defense by plants may or may not be the cause of the cycle, but Gullion will never be accused of a lack of creativity in trying to find the answer.

## PREDATOR-PREY RELATIONSHIPS

Yet another theory ties the cycle of the northern ruffed grouse to that of snowshoe hares, goshawks, and great horned owls. Grouse and snowshoe hares, of course, represent the two major prey species throughout much of the northern boreal forests. The other two species—goshawks and great horned owls—are the predominant predators of both hares and grouse in the region. Many biologists believe that when the populations of snowshoe hares are abundant, predators like hawks and owls prey chiefly on them, passing up a grouse dinner. The result is that grouse numbers climb until the hares exceed the carrying capacity of the habitat and decline. It is then that high concentrations of raptors turn to grouse for their livelihood. When grouse numbers plummet, the populations of avian predators also decline. Hare numbers are the first to recover, and they increase substantially faster than either grouse or raptor populations.

Dr. Donald Rusch, a grouse researcher from the Great Lakes region, has discovered that the snowshoe hare populations in Canada are directly linked to grouse numbers in the northern tier states. When hare populations decline in Canada, raptors move south in search of food. Their numbers are additive to existing populations of hawks and owls, so there is then abnormally high predation on ruffed grouse. This phenomenon may also trigger the downswing in the grouse cycle.

## THE DISPHARYNX DILEMMA

Ruffed grouse in northern regions are sometimes infected with a tiny roundworm parasite called dispharynx. In 1980, biologist Sue Marcquenski of the Wisconsin Department of Natural Resources (DNR) embarked on a long-term study of the parasite and how it was affecting grouse numbers.

Dispharynx burrow into the wall of a ruffed grouse's stomach and latch on tightly by using two threadlike projections called cordons. It's believed that these cordons act much the same as threads on a screw, securing the adult parasite to the stomach wall. An infected bird's stomach swells because of the extra tissue inside. This swelling commonly restricts the passage of food, thereby weakening the grouse and making it increasingly susceptible to illness and predation.

The grouse serves as the host to the parasite. Adult dispharynx pass their eggs out of the grouse via the grouse's fecal material. Once on the ground, the tiny eggs are ingested by sowbugs. Inside the sowbug, the young larvae begin to develop. When the sowbug is eaten by a grouse chick, the larvae grow to adults in the bird's stomach, and the cycle repeats itself.

In 1982, Marcquenski directed her efforts toward the grouse in Wisconsin's southwestern region. It was here that the state DNR had been live-trapping grouse to trade with Missouri for that state's wild turkey strain. Many of the grouse that were trapped and readied for shipment died before ever being sent. Dispharynx proved prevalent among the dead birds, and Marcquenski discovered that the coulee region of southwestern Wisconsin where the birds had been trapped showed a high concentration of the parasite—this, at a time when the region's grouse population was at a record ebb.

By graphing the relative number of ruffed grouse harvested from 1980 to 1983 and the number of infected grouse, Marcquenski showed what researchers call an inverse correlation. That is, as grouse populations decline, cases of dispharynx increase. But it was after she discovered the data from a 1937 study conducted by a Minnesota researcher that she made significant progress in further understanding the grouse's relationship with the dispharynx.

It's believed that the parasite will not actually kill ruffs outright but, like the phenols and tannins in aspen buds, will weaken them to the point where other factors such as cold weather and starvation can result in enough stress to kill the grouse. Aspen may produce their toxins when the grouse cycle is at its peak, so any grouse weakened by dispharynx may face a fatal dose of phenols or tannins— an amount that wouldn't normally kill a healthy bird.

Marcquenski's research is ongoing and may yet establish a definitive link between dispharynx and periodic swings in grouse populations.

# Early Birds

*Grouse are more than exciting; they are a rush, a blast of adrenalin straight through the nerves to the heart. NOTHING flushes like a ruffed grouse.*
　　　　　　　　　　　　　　　—Stephen J. Bodio, "Why Grouse"

# Early Birds

There are those who scoff at the thought of hunting grouse during the month of September: The leaves are still green and the cover is too thick; the weather's too hot and the dogs can't smell—and there are too many bugs. While a certain degree of truth lies behind these complaints, a person who would leave the dog in the kennel and the shotgun on the shelf during the grouse season simply cannot be called a grouse hunter. By mere definition, a grouse hunter spends nine months of the year in worship of the other three. Surely, a few mosquitos cannot deter such a pilgrim from the woods when there are grouse to be had?

But few people would consider my reasoning normal, and my judgment is highly suspect when it comes to grouse hunting. I have, without second thought, turned down numerous wedding invitations that fell between September and December. To the non-grouse hunter that is at best rude, at worst deplorable. But to a hell-bent, aspen-addicted partridge purist, the notion of attending a wedding—or any nonhunting social function—during the grouse season is absurd.

Over the years I have sought out equally corrupt individuals, and each fall we assemble to pay homage to *Bonasa umbellus*. We gather much the way southern dove hunters open the dove season, with a festive reverence centered around a general affection for ruffed grouse. Camp consists of a half-circle of tents with a campfire strategically located equidistant from each tent. Generally a pointer or two, wrapped in a circle, waits outside each tent. Grouse tails, tied to the tops of the tents, hang as not-so-subtle reminders of yesterday's profitable journey.

Hunts begin after the frost has melted from the aspen, but before it has dried. It is during this brief period that I would suppose a full 60 percent of the grouse I have taken over the years have succumbed. The moisture on the green leaves coupled with the cooling effect on the dogs seems to create an optimum scenting period. To further the equation, concentrate your efforts in areas which receive the first light in the morning: along the north sides of clearings where sunlight penetrates the southern edge of woods. The effect is this: After a chilly night, grouse dearly love to absorb the warming rays of the sun, and they are able to do it along the edge of cover that has grown thick because of the exposure to sunlight. Essentially, there is no more opportune time or place to hunt ruffed grouse.

It was my first setter who trained me—through countless repetitions—to gravitate toward these points of light. Invariably, his nose would eventually lead him to the habitat where all the right ingredients—sun, cover, and moisture—mixed. It is in these places and during these moments that most of my close encounters with grouse have occurred. Yet another virtue to stalking these green edges is that, occasionally, a grouse will choose to fly across an opening instead of leafward. If a hunter is fortunate enough to experience such a phenomenon, it is best to make the most of the shot because some time may elapse before such an opportunity arises again.

Birds of the early season are far more apt to tempt fate by exposing themselves to such vulnerabilities. Here lies one of the virtues of early season hunting. I often hear hunters retort by reciting the standard complaints about cover, weather, and bugs that encourage them to pass on early season grouse hunting, and I usually agree with them—not because I think they are at all correct, but rather because it leaves all the more grouse for me. I am, to be certain, a recluse when it comes to grouse hunting.

## UNDERSTANDING MORNING AND AFTERNOON HUNTS

My particular favorite of this litany of excuses to forego September grouse hunting is the suggestion that it is too hot for the dogs to scent properly. If you wait to begin your hunt at the convenient hour shortly after lunch, I suppose, it would be a bit warm on a typical September afternoon. But throughout the grouse's North American range, temperatures can vary widely during any given time of day. In the Great Lakes and Northeast states, temperatures at first light might be roughly 35 to 50 degrees Fahrenheit—certainly comfortable hunting temperature by most standards—but may climb as high as 80 degrees by late afternoon. Why not embark on an early morning hunt before breakfast?

During the early season, afternoons are meant for conversation while mornings are best spent frisking the coverts. A time-honored routine at my camp is to await the first ice-cube nose prodding and subsequent dose of dog breath from my setter in the morning. Dogs never awake at a civil hour; they stir when the forest does—the time that you should, too. First business is a hot fire and coffee that you would only drink in camp—the same sort of brew that would find its way down a drain in more civilized surroundings. Without wasting further grousing time, each of us forges off in separate directions for two, sometimes three, hours of hunting.

Upon returning to camp, a heaping brunch of leftover roasted grouse fillets, eggs, and slightly burnt toast completes a fulfilling morning. The dogs, wet with morning dew, find warm quarters in the sun where they curl up and rest. After feasting, the hunters do the same.

Late in the afternoon, perhaps an hour or two before sunset, we return to the aspen and alder for another look. By so doing, we are getting two different hunts each day. The character of the woods and of the birds themselves is remarkably different from morning to evening. We ask: Are these the same birds?

## ENJOYING ABUNDANT GROUSE

While differences show clearly in the complexions of a morning hunt and an afternoon hunt, an even greater transformation appears in the birds from early season to late. Perhaps the single greatest reason to hunt the early season is, quite simply, there are more grouse and fewer hunters. Prior to the grouse dispersal, the birds will be found in family groups. For the quail hunter accustomed to a covey of chances, this probably doesn't hold any unusual appeal, but to find three, four, five, or sometimes more grouse in one small covert is an event to be shared with the local barkeep. If he dares ask where you saw the birds, he is not a true grouse hunter; but if you tell him, neither are you.

Some hunters are under the impression that grouse numbers peak during the months of fall. In actuality, once chicks are hatched in May and June, the forest's population begins an inevitable decline as birds succumb to a wide assortment of factors including disease, predation, weather, and accidents. This continues, of course, until spring when the annual cycle of renewal in the forest once again gets underway. By postponing your hunting until the "leaves come off the trees" or "the bugs finally die," you forfeit the best grouse hunting of the year. To be sure, shooting in heavy cover more often resembles pruning, but if you seek birds and challenging wingshooting, there's little reason to wait. After all, shooting in cover is an inseparable, and integral, part of hunting ruffed grouse. Where, I ask, is the excitement if you are always able to see your target from the moment it flushes?

## KNOWING THE RIGHT COVER

Too many hunters, put in the midst of an aspen forest, wouldn't have even a faint clue about where to find grouse. While it is easy to simply say find aspen and, in all likelihood, you'll find grouse, there is much more to the matter. Grouse are far more particular about the cover they favor during the weeks of early fall. Indeed, aspen is to grouse what corn is to pheasant, but some stands of aspen are more appealing to grouse than others.

Early fall represents a time of bounty for the grouse, and finding food in the form of buds, seeds, berries, wild grapes, insects, acorns, and the like is scarcely as difficult as turning around. In years when the grouse cycle is on the upswing, even half-hearted jaunts through thick cover will reveal grouse. The mark of a skilled grouse hunter, however, is the ability to find grouse when the populations are down. An experienced hunter knows the difference between good cover and superb cover. In a down year, that will be the difference between finding grouse and simply taking a walk in the woods.

What, then, is "superb" cover? That was exactly what preeminent grouse researcher John Kubisiak of the Wisconsin Department of Natural Resources set out to discover. After years of conducting spring drumming censuses in the state in a variety of different age-classes of aspen, Kubisiak determined that aspen from six to twenty-six years old provided optimal conditions for ruffed grouse. Since aspen is a mainstay of the pulp industry throughout the Great Lakes region and many parts of New England, generally an abundance of such regrowth areas provides hunters with plenty of grouse-rich thickets.

Hunters who frequent the marginal habitat found on the fringe of the ruffed grouse range, however, are not so dependent upon regenerating stands of aspen to provide them with a huntable supply of grouse. My first encounter with Georgia grouse hunting, for example, was a lesson not only in geography but also in botany. It seemed amazing to me that these birds could find a niche in the mature oak forests of northern Georgia. It is, I should think, a tribute to the birds' adaptability. Early season hunts here are a test of patience. Bird densities in good years throughout much of the southern range are comparable to those found during low population levels in the Great Lakes or New England regions.

A small, cultlike band of southern hunters, however, has evolved to diligently chase grouse up and down the slopes of the southern Appalachian Mountains—typically late in the year, around December and January. Not until much of the leaf cover has fallen from the oak forests do the grouse congregate along the drainage bottoms, in junglelike thickets of holly and laurel. Even then, a one-bird day is a good day, and a two-bird day a cause for celebration. Many southern grouse hunters look upon the chance for a northern grouse hunt much the way Yanks revel at someday enjoying a plantation quail hunt. The mystique of both comes from not having experienced a hunt in a bird's prime range. It's a feeling as old as the nonresident license.

Whether hunting grouse north or grouse south, early season or late season, in aspen or in oak, grouse hunters share similar experiences. It is the intense anticipation of renewing friendships in the coverts, of awaiting a young bird dog's first introduction to grouse hunting, and of marveling at the sights, sounds, and smells of a woods promising grouse.

# Late, Great Grouse

*Doves test our marksmanship, pheasants our tenacity, and Huns our legs, but the ruffed grouse tests all of these—and more.*

—Steve Smith, *Hunting Upland Birds*

# Late, Great Grouse

I expect the grouse from the orchard covert to flush past the windmill and over the red pines to Brown's Coulee as every grouse that has ever come from that covert has always done. I go to great pains to be in position to shoot at the bird that I know will be flying—more or less—in line with its predecessors. Then, of course, the bird chooses instead to fly north, over Straight's Hill toward the abyss of uncharted coverts.

I stand there, mouth agape, and wonder why this bird selected a different course. After recreating the scenario in my mind and scanning my surroundings, I come to realize that this is the first time I have hunted the orchard covert so late in the year. Why, of course! The reason the bird didn't head toward Brown's Coulee as it or its kin had done earlier in the year is that Brown's Coulee now offers nothing more than a leafless stand of trees, giving little protection to the bird. During the early season, however, the grouse favored the security of the coulee because a dense layer of crimson sumac leaves still provided a protective solarium for the birds.

## CHANGING SEASONS, CHANGING COVER

Coverts begin an inexorable change from the moment the first dry leaf blows landward. I've often wondered what it would be like to be a grouse watching my favorite thicket of poplar dissolve around me, leaf by precious leaf. For the yearling grouse, what a wholly unnerving experience to watch a gust of wind blow a shower of spent leaves upon it. Imagine the roof of your house, then the walls of your abode, simply drifting down to the foundation. It's little wonder the birds seek out fermented grapes and imbibe the fruits of fall.

The difference between an early season grouse hunt and a late season one is often the difference between success and failure for hunters who don't learn to adapt with the grouse. Ruffs are a transitional species that moves to the best cover throughout the year. While you may find them in a given location during September and October, they may relocate to an entirely different covert by November. Some of this movement is a natural tendency to seek out the best available cover, while the rest can be explained by a phenomenon known as dispersal—an event beginning in fall and often continuing through spring.

Dispersal for grouse can be equated to graduation for humans. It's a time of many transitions in life. When young grouse reach roughly their four-month birthday, they begin a search for homes of their own. While most drummers remain within one or two miles of their brood site, hens typically range farther. In a Minnesota study under the direction of grouse authority Gordon Gullion, a radio-tagged female was found over ten miles from her brood site! That is a remarkable feat when we consider that most of the hen's journey was done on foot. To equate this to a human undertaking, let's suppose that each step a grouse takes is roughly three inches long. Considering that this grouse very likely didn't take a direct course to reach her final destination, this marathon bird took a minimum of 211,200 steps—excluding any short flights—to cover the ten miles. Now, suppose that an average human gait is 2½ feet. Taking the same number of steps that the grouse did, a human would have traveled one hundred miles. If you find this astonishing, be informed that yet another grouse was documented to have traveled seventy-one miles from its brood site during dispersal!

Generally speaking, grouse are much like humans in that they want a roof over their heads—some, as you can see, will go to great lengths to find a suitable roof. A roof, in this case, may be nothing more than a toppled tree or other windfall. Biologists refer to this as horizontal cover. While grouse favor vertical cover in the form of aspen shoots and other stems when leaves remain on the trees, they often choose horizontal habitat when the protective canopy of leaves no longer hangs overhead and there isn't suitable snow cover to provide shelter in the form of snow tunnels.

## HUNTING WINTER COVER

I was first exposed to the virtues of hunting deadfalls and brush piles during the most memorable grouse hunt I've ever experienced. It took place in 1979 in western Wisconsin, not far from the Minnesota border. That winter was uncharacteristically dry, with scarcely a dusting of snow on the ground. I was hunting an area where several small stands of oaks had been razed to undoubtedly become kitchen tables somewhere in a Chicago suburb. The trees had been felled sometime in September, and the remaining slash was haphazardly heaped hither and yon through the woods. Since the trees had been cut so early in the year when the leaves were growing and firmly attached, the leaves remained on the slash, providing a cozy, insulated hideout for the grouse. Normally, though, the birds would have preferred to burrow into the snow where their newly created tunnels allow them to conserve much of their body heat. Winter survival is little more than energy conservation for grouse as every wasted calorie can mean the difference between life and death.

The ruffed grouse is, however, a creature well adapted to surviving winter. Scalelike pectinations on a grouse's feet and feathers that extend like a warm pant leg all the way to the base of its feet give ample indication that these birds are creatures of the North. The minute scales on a grouse's feet give the bird's toes a centipede appearance. Biologists believe that these pectinations are used to help grouse grip icy tree branches while they feed on aspen catkins and other buds. Such small adaptations can be critical in what can best be called a precarious existence during the winter months.

I think of winter's unforgiving nature toward wildlife each time I sally forth on a late season hunt, for hunters don't necessarily have to shoot grouse outright to cause their demise. Hunters who stalk the woodlands for grouse during the late season carry with them a burden of responsibility. It comes in the knowledge that each time a grouse is forced to take flight and leave its sheltering roost, the bird exposes itself to a gauntlet of predators—one of the deadliest of all being unforgiving winter weather. "A grouse in flight is usually a grouse in trouble," wrote Gullion when assessing the potential dangers to a ruffed grouse when it's forced to flee.

I would hazard to say that a grouse hunter's greatest skill lies not in his proficiency at killing grouse, rather in his ability at recognizing the difference between a healthy and an ailing covert. The same spirit of stewardship keeps quail hunters from blasting a covey until too few birds remain to collectively withstand the elements. This consciousness of the coverts becomes increasingly important each year grouse tailspin in their decade-long cycle.

But during the bountiful years of the cycle—roughly years six through ten—hunter impact is often negligible by virtue of supply and demand. Such was the case when, in roughly four hours of hunting these oak brushpiles, my brother and I along with one setter encountered over fifty grouse, having lost count during our umpteenth flush. To be sure, many of these flushes were second encounters, but they were flushes nevertheless. With a peaked population cycle and a combination of factors causing the grouse to congregate, it was much like a trout angler matching the hatch the precise moment a stream begins to boil with hungry browns.

This hunt illustrates the importance of locating cover that offers grouse protection from both cold temperatures and avian predators, goshawks and great horned owls. Remember that thick stands of even 15,000 stems-per-acre in October may be veritable deserts for grouse come December. Even aspen that is normally considered prime age for grouse—six to twenty-five years—will seldom hold grouse with the onset of winter unless there is a layer of powdery snow at least ten inches deep or an abundance of deadfalls and other forms of horizontal cover.

One cover component meeting this criterion for ample late season habitat is young-growth evergreens. Although the many layers of interwoven branches on mature conifers may harbor predators, young trees offer an attractive alternative when the woods are void of an insulating layer of snow. Pine, spruce, and fir become a bit of an oasis for grouse and can be exceptionally productive when they are located near mature stands of poplar, the catkins of which provide the major source of protein for wintering grouse.

Although often productive, hunting in evergreen groves can be a cross between pulling weeds and taking a cold shower. Pine boughs in dense stands of young trees typically form a nearly impenetrable barrier a few feet off the ground, so traversing such zones is a matter of walking hunched-over in a posture similar to one used to weed the garden. The same pine needles that offer protection to grouse commonly hold a coating of snow that inevitably finds its way down your back as you traipse the evergreens. In this case, however, rewards are often commensurate with suffering.

There is nothing sophisticated about hunting ruffed grouse in pine thickets. It's grouse hunting reduced to trench warfare. Sane hunters wouldn't so much as consider venturing into such surroundings—that is, of course, unless they hadn't seen a grouse in several hours. This, you might have guessed, was precisely what had happened to me.

My foolhardy setter—a beast I am convinced knows more about ruffed grouse than all the doctors of grouseology who ever counted droppings in an aspen thicket—was the first to introduce me to the joys of grousing in pine groves. It happened by chance. While we hunted the hill country of southwestern Wisconsin, a remarkably thick layer of fog settled over Richland County. That wouldn't have been altogether bad except that I was somewhere within Richland County—the question was, Where? I was lost. But only temporarily, I convinced myself.

I spent the better part of the day roaming the hills, unsuccessfully searching for grouse. After climbing two hills that I was certain would bring me to my pickup, I found nothing but another empty valley, no vehicle in sight. "It isn't as though I am in the middle of a wilderness," I told myself. "I just have to walk in one direction until I hit a road. At worst, there's always a milk truck on the highway each morning." I favored this possibility after concluding that I was too damn tired to try to backtrack my way over the hills.

Somewhere between my pickup and Iowa, my setter ambled into a small stand of what looked to be overgrown Christmas trees. The ensuing thunderous flushes were small compensation for my predicament. I hopped to a small knoll that overlooked the red pine stand that couldn't have been more than twenty by forty yards in size. It is virtually impossible to walk the pines and expect to get shooting at escaping birds. The pine boughs were far too thick for me to negotiate without crawling on my hands and knees, so I let my setter enjoy his beaglelike rendition of running circles under the pines. After less than ten minutes, he spooked thirteen grouse from the trees—three flew a course squarely into my number eights. The fact that only now can I write in good humor about this adventure is testimony to the value of a compass being permanently placed in your hunting vest. I only wish I had remembered the device six hills earlier.

# In Mixed Company

*The neophyte grouser goes to the woods hoping to find game. The knowledgeable grouse hunter enters the woods knowing he's going to flush his share of ruffs.*
—Nick Sisley, *Grouse & Woodcock*

# In Mixed Company

O nly after I experienced my first earthquake had I discovered an event similar to a grouse flush. A ruff catapulting from underfoot would likely register somewhere between 5.5 and 6.2 on the Richter scale. A launching woodcock, on the other hand, is a mere tremor by comparison. But hunting the two in concert is a wholly exhilarating experience whose hallmark is anticipation. It is the supreme test not only of shooter and dog, but also of blood pressure.

## HUNTING SOUTHERN STYLE

It wasn't until I moved to Atlanta to edit a chain of outdoor magazines that I came to realize how utterly stupendous my grousing and woodcocking was in the Midwest. The weathered, oak-covered hills of northern Georgia provide a spectacular backdrop for grouse hunters. They are a pleasant and needed diversion when the grouse hunting is slow—and that is often. Georgia presented a stark contrast to the type of grouse and woodcock hunting I had grown accustomed to in the Great Lakes states.

Unlike the hunting in the North where grouse and woodcock are commonly found occupying the same habitat, the two birds in the South seldom inhabit the same ecotone. The grouse in Georgia, for instance, are rarely found below 1,500 feet of elevation. Woodcock, on the other hand, are located almost entirely in the moist bottomlands adjacent to riverbeds, often surrounded by stands of Spanish moss-draped loblolly pines. Southern woodcock hunting shares little similarity with the hunting found in southern Canada, the Great Lakes area, and New England states.

Since northern Georgia lies at the southern fringe of the grouse range, biologists believe that the lower temperatures of the higher elevations more closely mimic conditions found in the birds' prime range to the north. Biologist Kent Kammermeyer of the Georgia Department of Natural Resources says that plant species important to southern grouse are seldom found below 2,000 feet of elevation. Primary food and cover types include mountain laurel, honeysuckle, greenbrier, rhododendron, and American holly. Hunters will also find grouse near thickets of dogwood and sassafras berry. Shortly after I moved to Dixie, a well-seasoned southern grouse hunter began my introduction to grouse hunting below the Mason-Dixon Line by instructing me to hunt near stands of holly and laurel.

Further north lies Tennessee, which shares many biotic similarities with northern Georgia, but does sport slightly better grouse populations. Jim Little of the Tennessee Wildlife Resources Division has enjoyed years of grouse and woodcock hunting in eastern Tennessee. Little is an honorary member of the illustrious Woodcock Mossgauge Benevolent Society, a group of several hundred fanatical woodcock hunters who rendezvous across the country each fall to exchange lies and share hunts. It is very likely group therapy for people who spend much of their falls traipsing through tangled swamps in search of a tiny six-ounce bird with a long beak and goofy eyes. These folks are undoubtedly descendants of a long line of *snipe* hunters.

Hunters like Little find their best hunting in the Appalachian Mountains east of the Cumberland Plateau in eastern Tennessee. Here, as in Georgia, the higher elevations share many of the same plant species important to grouse, like mountain laurel, rhododendron, and holly. Downslope, adjacent to stream bottoms are likely locations for migrating woodcock. Over the last twenty years, however, the eastern woodcock population has experienced a precipitous decline at a rate of 3 percent per year.

## IMPROVING EASTERN HABITAT

Woodcock exist east of a line beginning in eastern Manitoba and extending due south to Louisiana. Within that range exist two distinct populations of woodcock: an eastern flock and a western flock. It is the timberdoodles of the eastern range—beginning in Labrador and extending south down the Atlantic seaboard—that have biologists particularly concerned. Studies conducted at the Moosehorn National Wildlife Refuge in Maine indicate that this trend in diminishing population is reversible, but that a solution will take cooperation between governmental and private sectors. Unfortunately, with increased international emphasis being placed on waterfowl restoration, the plight of the woodcock has gone largely unnoticed by bureaucrats in Washington, D.C.

The decline in woodcock numbers throughout the eastern range is largely caused by a proliferation of over-mature forests. Woodcock are birds of young, moist forests. Since the majority of eastern forests lies in private hands, private landowners play a critical role in replenishing woodcock numbers. It is a matter of continually harvesting small parcels of the forest to create the new-growth forests so important to the welfare of woodcock.

Research at Moosehorn indicates that woodcock also need scattered forest openings, for here male woodcocks undertake their spring courtship display. These areas also provide feeding grounds for woodcock. To accomplish this, researchers have cleared strips of woodlands seventy by two hundred feet in size next to stands four times that scope. By continually cropping aspen stands in a grid pattern, biologists are able to keep a constant supply of prime habitat types for woodcock. Meanwhile, the harvested timber is used to fuel local pulp mills. Researchers reported an unprecedented 500 percent increase in woodcock populations after such habitat manipulation was undertaken!

The commercial viability of aspen as an important source of pulp is critical to any plans of improving eastern woodcock habitat. Aspen is to grouse and woodcock what corn and other grains are to pheasant. Just as the pheasant does best when grain fields are small and well interspersed with hedgerows and grasslands, so grouse and woodcock fare best when aspen clear-cuts are small, offering a variety of aspen in different stages of growth. Ten- to twenty-acre clear-cuts of aspen are far more beneficial to grouse and woodcock than are huge commercial cuts sometimes encompassing several hundred acres. Because of public outcry over these huge clear-cuts that left a scarred landscape, many states now mandate that timber harvesters not exceed a given number of acres in each clear-cut. Such laws have been an ecological boon for many wildlife species dependent upon diversity in the forest biota.

The view while flying over the small clear-cut strips in Moosehorn looks similar to the upland mosaic of small farm plots commonly found in the East. It's difficult to imagine such intensive habitat management ever taking hold on a wide scale, but with the decline of eastern pheasant, quail, and waterfowl populations, the woodcock once scoffed at by some has become a prized gamebird for many.

This is particularly true in years when grouse populations are at cyclic ebbs. Although grouse throughout the South do not show the same kind of cyclic tendency as their northern counterparts, their populations do fluctuate in an irregular pattern. During peak years in Tennessee, six to ten grouse flushes per day will keep most hunters happy, while West Virginia hunters do slightly better than that. Georgia grousers, on the other hand, rarely experience such grousing opportunities. Indeed, there are no more dedicated souls than Georgia grouse hunters—and their ranks can be counted quickly.

## THE PERFECT COMPLEMENT

A walk in a grouse woods after woodcock have left for their migratory trail can be a lonely experience. A grouse hunter rejoices when the aspen and alder are shared with woodcock. But to make such a statement is to prejudice the importance of woodcock. After all, in the era of equal rights, it could as easily be said that, "A *woodcock* hunter rejoices when the aspen and alder are shared with *grouse.*" Nevertheless, woodcock are most often the "mix" in a grouse hunter's mixed bag—the tonic in a gin drink. But then the full flavor of the experience is lost if one ingredient is missing.

Such musings occupy my mind at the end of a hunt, setter resting comatose with his chin on my knee, sun beaming through the aspens as I lean against a decaying oak, surveying the area from which I have just walked. I don't know how many ill-fated, woeful grouse hunts have been rescued by the sudden twitter of woodcock wings. I often wonder if God placed woodcock on the earth to keep grouse hunters and grouse dogs from losing all confidence. With all due respect to the diminutive bird, I sometimes think woodcock are living proof that God has a sense of humor. Here is a bird with a Pinnochio-like beak, toothpick legs, and bulging eyes. It appears an upland oddball, a biological misfit left over from some mixed-up evolutionary gene pool. Yet, it is remarkably adapted to life in the forest.

The eyes of a woodcock are set far back in its head, allowing it to view approaching predators in a 360-degree radius. The ears are set forward in the head, in front of the eyes and closer to the ground—a handy adaptation when finding worms is your livelihood. In fact, a woodcock will devour up to two times its weight in worms every day. The crawlers are quickly converted to energy to support the high metabolism of the woodcock, and whatever the seven- or eight-inch body doesn't utilize becomes drops of white-out on the forest floor. These tiny paint splashes, along with a preponderance of overturned leaves, are telltale indications that woodcock are nearby.

Invariably, the moment I notice woodcock chalk on fallen alder or aspen leaves,

When there isn't enough snow on the ground for grouse to tunnel for warmth, they seek out thickets of heavy cover or, occasionally, evergreen stands. (*Photo © by Chris Dorsey*)

Overgrown orchards dot the hills of some New England and Midwest states and often provide suitable habitat for grouse. (*Photo © by Bob Robb*)

Aspen and other tree buds often compose a primary source of protein for wintering grouse in the north country. (*Photo © by Tom Martinson*)

Grouse become increasingly skittish as the season progresses. Their running abilities will never be compared to that of a pheasant, but they will commonly elude hunters by electing to run instead of fly. (*Photo © by Herb Lange*)

A grouse that launches from a tree branch when a hunter approaches is quite likely a bird that will live another day. (*Photo © by Herb Lange*)

Male grouse occasionally drum in the fall. These drummers may be the young of the year seeking to establish their own domain in the forest or well-seasoned birds looking to protect their territory from the intruding youngsters. (*Photo © by John Kubisiak*)

When a grouse climbs atop a log to drum he is, in effect, also advertising to predators. Indeed, when the leaves fall from the trees, hawks and owls are treated to Thanksgiving. (*Photo* © *by Herb Lange*)

Throughout much of the grouse's range east of the Mississippi, woodcock cohabitate. Given the difference in flight speeds between the two birds in the thick coverts both birds inhabit, you are sure to have, well, interesting shooting. (*Photo © by Rob Robb*)

It is a rare grouse dog that can consistently point both grouse and woodcock. Such dogs are a mix of good breeding, experience, and divine intervention. (*Photo © by Bob Robb*)

One of the splendors of hunting both grouse and woodcock is that you're never sure if the next flush will be a ruff or a timberdoodle. In this anticipation converges much of the pleasure of grouse and woodcock hunting. (*Photo* © *by Chris Dorsey*)

The extended neck ruff and complete tail band are good indications that this grouse is, indeed, a male. (*Photo © by Tom Martinson*)

A ruffed grouse seen nesting can only be a female, while a drumming grouse is certainly a male. In grouse, unlike in other species, males never share nesting duties with females. (*Photo © by Tom Martinson*)

Though the grouse on the left has a broken tail band, other physical features indicate that the bird is a male, as is the grouse on the right. (*Photo © by Chris Dorsey*)

Biologist John Kubisiak determines the sex and age of a grouse during a banding operation at Wisconsin's Sandhill Experimental Wildlife Area. (*Photo © by Dave Otto*)

This male grouse was intrigued by the put-put noise of a golf cart used to carry a film crew to a new location during the taping of a public television nature series. Cinematographer Marshall Savick gets a bird's-eye view as the grouse leaves his roost to investigate the crew. (*Photo © by Dan Small*)

Instructional videos and television programs continue to inform hunters about the latest trends in wildlife management and hunting opportunities. The author (*right*) describes the process of aging a ruffed grouse to Dan Small, host of the Public Broadcasting System series "Outdoor Wisconsin," during a late season outing. (*Photo © by Chuck Petrie*)

I also discover the absence of the sound of Thor's bell . . . point! Woodcock will never be known as running birds, at least not in the same sense as chukars or pheasants. Their most reliable defense is their mottled camouflage. Upon hearing an oncoming threat, the birds simply plunk down amongst the litter of leaves and wait for the danger to pass. More often than not, their camouflage serves them well. Thanks to the olfactory wizardry of Thor and countless dogs like him, however, over two million woodcock are taken each year during the four million individual hunter days spent pursuing the bird in North America.

As Leopold wrote in his now immortalized *A Sand County Almanac*, "When at last he [your dog] stops stock-still, and says with a sideward glance, 'Well, get ready,' the question is, ready for what? A twittering woodcock, or the rising roar of a grouse, or perhaps only a rabbit? In this moment of uncertainty is condensed much of the virtue of grouse hunting. He who must know what to get ready for should go and hunt pheasants."

# How to Be a Feather Sleuth

*What is a country without rabbits and partridges?*

—Henry David Thoreau

# How to Be a Feather Sleuth

## SEXING GROUSE

Of all the game birds on our continent, ruffed grouse are perhaps among the most difficult in which to determine sex. Sexing grouse allows a hunter to gain a greater understanding of the birds stalked. Is the dead log ten paces from where you last shot a grouse the old cock's drumming stage? Will another male find the stump to continue the ageless, winged drum roll? The difficulty in aging grouse is particularly evident when hearing the misinformation many hunters recite in their attempt to distinguish the difference between the two sexes. My favorite, however, was from a deer hunter I encountered while grouse hunting north of Banff National Park in Alberta, Canada.

"The gray birds are the males," he said with confidence, "and the brown ones are the hens, eh."

"I don't think that's very reliable, sir," I replied.

"Oh ya, yes they are. . . . I read it once somewhere," he insisted.

After several unsuccessful attempts to convince him otherwise, I ambled back through the clear-cut from which I came.

"Remember," I added with a smirk before departing, "the does are the deer with antlers."

Despite the occasional hunter who holds dear such misbegotten folk beliefs, most hunters are accustomed to using a grouse's tail band to determine sex. While it is possible to get a reasonable guess as to whether a bird is male or female using this method, it is far from infallible. The majority of male birds, of course, will have a continual dark band across the fringe of the tail. Hens, on the other hand, typically have a broken band in the center of the tail fan. However, roughly 25 percent of male grouse will also have a broken tail band.

A more reliable, albeit more complex, method is to measure the length of the center tail feathers. Though there is a certain degree of regional variance, if a fully fledged grouse's middle tail feathers are longer than $5\frac{7}{8}$ inches, the bird is a male. Tail feathers less than $5\frac{1}{2}$ inches indicate the bird is female. This method, however, also has its shortcomings: It only works if the birds are mature with fully developed feathers, and since most hunters don't carry a ruler afield, it does little for field identification.

Early in the hunting season when immature birds are common, I prefer to use eyepatch color as a determining factor. Both males and females have a small bare patch of skin directly above the eye. A male's eyepatch is usually a dull orange during the months of fall while a hen's will typically have no color at all. As with all methods of distinguishing the sexes, biologists first verified their theories of the sexes by comparing them to the grouse's internal organs—the only truly definitive method of sexing ruffed grouse.

Another sound way to field judge the differences between male and female grouse is to use the white spots on the bird's rump feathers. If a rump feather of a grouse has two or more white spots on its tip, it is most likely a male. If, however, the rump feather has but one white dot, chances are that it is a female.

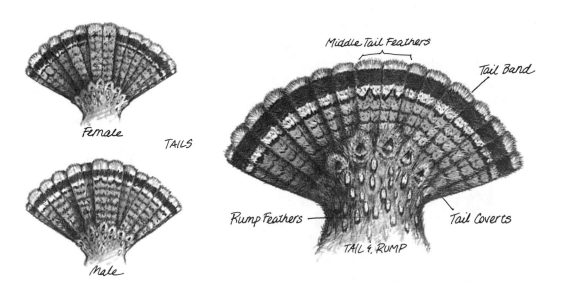

These methods seem straightforward, and for the most part, they are. But confusion sets in when grouse exhibit both male and female characteristics. For example, suppose a grouse has two dots on its rump feathers and a middle tail feather measuring roughly six inches (the length of a dollar bill), characteristics which indicate a male. The same grouse, however, also had the female characteristics of a broken tail band and no coloration in its eyepatch. Recall that 25 percent of all males have a broken tail band and, according to a Minnesota study, 2.5 percent of all males have no coloration in their eyepatch. The key, then, is to determine which methods of sexing grouse are the most reliable.

By comparing conclusions from external observation with results from internal sexing by biologists, here in descending order is a ranking from most reliable to least conclusive methods of sexing grouse: 1. internal examination of testes and ovaries, 2. length of tail and wing feathers, 3. dots on rump feathers, 4. eyepatch, and 5. tail band. Given the above example, the statistical probability of the grouse being a male is greater since the characteristics designating it as a male—rump dots and tail feather length—have proven more reliable than either the broken tail band or colorless eyepatch.

## THE AGE-OLD QUESTION

How old is that grouse? Although you may have pondered this question as you examined a bird taken, in all practicality it is a difficult question to answer beyond simply distinguishing juveniles from adult birds. At first glance, juvenile birds may seem indistinguishable from adults, but the simplest way to tell the difference is by their development of primary feathers.

These primaries—also called flight feathers—follow a predictable pattern of molt and growth, thus allowing for accurate age estimates in young birds. The total number of these feathers is ten. They are numbered starting with one at the smallest feather at the base of the wing and extending to number ten at the wing tip. The innermost primary is the first to be molted and is sequentially followed by two, three, four, and so forth. As more feathers fall out, the initial primaries to drop are already being replaced. Juveniles molt all but the ninth and tenth primaries, while adults molt all ten primaries. In either case, however, the birds do not lose their power of flight.

It is this fact that adults molt all of their flight feathers that makes it possible to distinguish between the two age groups. The ninth and tenth primaries are usually fully grown by the time most hunting seasons open. If the last two feathers on

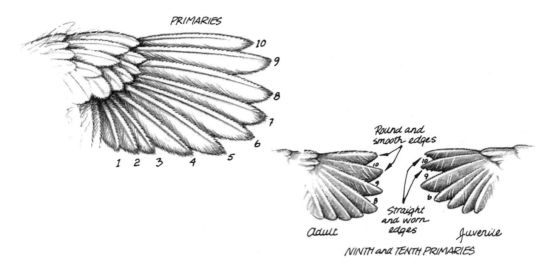

PRIMARIES

10
9
8
7
6
5
1  2  3    4

Round and
smooth edges

Straight
and worn
edges

Adult                    Juvenile

NINTH and TENTH PRIMARIES

both wings happen to be growing, however, it is a likely sign that the bird is an adult.

Examine the trailing edges of the ninth and tenth primaries near their outer tips. If the edges are smooth and sloped, they are likely the newly grown feathers of an adult. The last two primaries of a juvenile will be straight and worn from extended use. This isn't always simple to distinguish, so another clue that can help in your determination is the presence of a sheath around the primary feathers.

A fully developed feather will have the sheathing on its quill end for a while. The sheath is clear and flaky, much as if a thin layer of skin is dried and peeling off the quill. The more recent the feather's growth, the more sheathing that will be on the quill. You can compare the amount of residual sheathing between the ninth and eighth primaries by pulling them out and examining their respective quills. Since primary eight is replaced annually, there will always be at least a minimal amount of sheathing on the feather during the fall. If the ninth primary has the same amount of sheathing on it that primary eight has, it is a new feather—indicative of an adult. If the ninth flight feather has little if any sheathing compared to the eighth primary, odds are that it is an old feather from a juvenile.

Hunters can use this information to determine the ratios of adults to juveniles in their favorite coverts. In healthy grouse populations, juveniles will always out-number adults. If you harvest more adults than juveniles, most likely something has gone awry in the flock. It may indicate, for instance, that the late winter snows and the cold, wet spring hampered nesting success, which in turn reduced the number of birds that made it to the fall. From this information, prudent hunters adjust their hunting accordingly.

# Are We Over-Gunning Grouse?

*It's one thing to drill a sitting grouse before it flies, but quite another to shoot a bird that won't fly, even after verbal abuse.*

*—David Carty, "Grouse Of A Different Color"*

# Are We Over-Gunning Grouse?

Does legal hunting impact overall game populations? That was an exam question in a wildlife management course I took several years ago during my days as a collegian. Almost everyone in the class of 180 students knew that hunting didn't affect overall game numbers. That, of course, was the widely accepted axiom of the day. Aldo Leopold, Durward Allen, and other noted wildlife biologists had published reams of documents to support just such a claim. But the times, like the dynamics of hunting, are changing.

## EXTENDED HUNTING SEASONS

Researchers in Pennsylvania and Wisconsin have suspected for some time and now are learning that human hunters may, indeed, take heavy tolls on isolated populations of ruffed grouse. Biologists in Pennsylvania began a study in 1982 to determine the effect of extended hunting seasons on grouse numbers and harvests.

They began by closing the grouse season early in select counties. By comparing these harvest and flush rates with those in counties that remained open through January, biologists developed an understanding of the impact of extended hunting opportunities on grouse survival. Select hunters were surveyed to develop an average of the number of flushes each experienced as well as the number of birds bagged in a single hunt.

While statewide grouse populations were climbing out of a cyclic low at the time of the study, they didn't increase as rapidly in the counties where late season hunting was permitted. Moreover, in a published report, biologist John Kriz wrote, "The closed counties flushing rates have increased slightly more than have the comparable open counties.... The most interesting changes concern a slightly lower percent of juveniles in the comparable open counties and slightly lower flush rate increase in these same counties. If these trends continue and enlarge in coming seasons it could mean grouse populations may be affected by the extended hunting season."

## INCREASED HARVESTS AND LOST HABITATS

It is important to account for other variables that affect grouse populations in addition to season length. The Wisconsin study, conducted throughout the 1980s, did just that. Dr. Donald Rusch of the University of Wisconsin has made a career out of studying grouse and has found astounding results from his studies in Wisconsin.

When reviewing harvest figures derived from hunter surveys, Rusch was surprised by the continued increase in recent grouse harvests in Wisconsin. His review of annual surveys taken during the late 1980s indicated that over one million grouse had been taken by hunters in the state. That is a large sum, said Rusch in a published report, considering it would mean that an average of forty-four grouse were taken off each section of Wisconsin's 23,000 square miles of forest. Of course, not all that forest is suitable grouse habitat, so it's likely that far more than forty-four grouse are being taken off sections in the state's best grouse range. By comparison, Wisconsin biologists estimate that the average section of the state's forest supports a total of somewhere between fifty and one hundred grouse during the fall.

Rusch conducted similar calculations for harvests-per-section in Michigan and Minnesota and wound up with thirty-five and forty-five grouse respectively. Could these figures be accurate? After considerable consultation and debate with other prominent ruffed grouse biologists, including Gordon Gullion of Minnesota and Walt Palmer of Michigan, Rusch concluded that the figures were probably accurate. From these figures, Rusch drew the implication that a significantly large percentage of grouse-per-section was being shot. If the numbers were accurate, they would indicate a harvest too large for the overall health of these states' grouse.

In Wisconsin, some biologists believe that declining pheasant and duck populations may be steering more hunters toward the woodlands instead of the sloughs. This, combined with the sharp increase in hunter numbers since the 1940s and 1950s—when Leopold and Allen published much of their landmark wildlife management literature—has contributed to the increase in grouse harvests. It's likely that this trend is being experienced in many states where grouse have maintained stronger populations than have other upland game and waterfowl. In addition, grouse seasons and bag limits are, in many states, as liberal as they have been since the abolishment of unregulated market hunting.

Liberal hunting regulations, again, largely result from the belief that hunting has little if any impact on grouse populations. This notion is based on the fact that over 50 percent of the birds will die each year whether hunted by humans or not. Also, it was commonly understood that few birds were being taken at the hands of people anyway and that grouse populations were cyclic regardless of hunter pressure.

Beginning with the decade of the 1980s, however, many areas in Wisconsin have been experiencing heavy hunting pressure, and there's little doubt that it is affecting grouse populations in these intensively hunted areas. This increase in hunting is coupled significantly with a decrease in grouse habitat. Much of the Great Lakes states' best grouse range is found where aspen is the predominant forest species. Since aspen must either be harvested for pulp or burned roughly every forty years to continue as viable grouse habitat, it's important that loggers develop markets for the aspen. Otherwise, the aspen forest gives way to the next successional stage of pines—which are nearly useless for grouse and many other species of forest wildlife.

Ironically, some midwestern pulp mill operators are looking to South American growers to provide them with eucalyptus logs that can be imported at less expense than local loggers can supply home-grown aspen. This has meant that more acres of aspen are being left to mature in our forests, with the end result being a decline in grouse numbers. Rusch reports that, "In Wisconsin, grouse numbers have probably declined over the past four decades as grouse habitats have also declined."

The upshot is that, at present, there are more hunters on fewer acres of grouse habitat. It seems apparent that the increasing grouse harvest must be curtailed on areas where human hunting pressure threatens the birds' existence. To determine where some of those areas might be, Rusch and other state biologists, in cooperation with the Wisconsin Department of Natural Resources and the Ruffed Grouse Society, undertook a series of additional studies designed specifically to determine just how many birds were being taken by hunters in select areas of the state.

Rusch and a team of researchers chose two heavily hunted wildlife management areas in Wisconsin to begin their study in the mid-1980s: Sandhill and Navarino. John Kubisiak, a biologist stationed at Sandhill, "live-trapped and banded 713 grouse on areas open to hunting," said Rusch, and "an incredible 304 (42 percent) were taken during the hunting season! In 1980–81, when grouse numbers and hunter interest were near a peak at Sandhill, hunters took more than 60 percent of the grouse marked on the hunted portion." Although Navarino didn't experience harvest rates as high as those at Sandhill, they were still higher than expected with nearly one-quarter of the banded birds being taken by hunters during the three-month season. Biologists were stunned at the findings. What's more, these are underestimates of the actual harvest because not all of the birds killed are reported and some of the banded birds died of causes other than hunting by humans. In fact, biologist Steve DeStefano of Navarino calculated that the harvest rate might be 50 percent higher than the recovery rate of the banded birds. This means that in some areas upwards of 90 percent of a given grouse population is being taken by human hunters.

Biologists in other parts of the state scrambled to confirm the findings and once again reported alarmingly high harvest rates on other of the state's public hunting areas. In a study in Marquette and Waushara counties, 25 percent of banded grouse were reported harvested by hunters. "This band recovery rate is surprisingly high considering that many of these grouse dispersed from the narrow corridors of public land to nearby, posted property," observed Rusch.

Biologists were able to determine, Rusch continued, that if a bird spent the entire hunting season on public lands, its probability of being shot was an astounding 92 percent! If, however, a grouse spent the season on nearby private land, presumably hunted less than publicly owned property because of limited access, its probability of being shot was only 6 percent.

The challenge now is to discover how widespread this overharvest is and to develop management plans to effectively reduce grouse harvests on areas where hunting pressure may be stressing grouse populations. Grouse biologists around the country will be watching the results of both the Wisconsin and Pennsylvania studies because we may be seeing the dawn of a trend in some of our grouse coverts.

As Rusch warned: "We cannot afford to ignore the consequences and implications of high harvest rates in ruffed grouse. Grouse that live in forest remnants in landscapes dominated by man are especially vulnerable to the effects of heavy harvest. The disappearance of grouse from Arkansas, Missouri, Illinois, and parts of Kentucky, Tennessee and southern Wisconsin is probably due to excessive exploitation of isolated populations."

# The Ruffed Grouse Society

*I shot a ruffed grouse about 300 yards behind it [a dead elm], flushed from a patch of wild blackberry bushes in late November. . . . I have been hunting that country for 25 years now. It never used to be posted this way. Now I come in from the backside, from the next dirt road north where there are only 27 NO HUNTING signs per mile. You can accidentally walk in between those.*

*—Ron Rau, "U Keep Out"*

# The Ruffed Grouse Society

S ince its modest beginning on October 24, 1961, the Ruffed Grouse Society (RGS) has grown from a fledgling conservation organization to one encompassing a wide assortment of programs that ultimately benefit many forest wildlife species—not simply ruffed grouse and woodcock.

As the story of the founding of the organization is told in the society's bulletin, "On a fall day in 1961 in Monterey, Virginia, Seybert Beverage, attorney, met in his office with Bruce R. Richardson, Jr., and Dixie L. Shumate, Jr. When business obligations had been satisfied, the talk in Beverage's office turned to the upcoming hunting season and to the ruffed grouse." The conversations of these men gave birth to the society. It is a classic story of sportsmen building the backbone of wildlife conservation in America, of hunters feeling compelled to put something back. The three founders of the organization weren't sure what had to be done, but they knew depressed grouse populations would not rebound unless first given a chance. Forests spared the wrath of fires and timber harvests were outgrowing their ability to support many wildlife species like ruffed grouse.

## MANAGING GROUSE HABITAT

A small newsletter was established to serve as a clearinghouse for information about the ruffed grouse and as a vehicle for communications between members. The focus of the organization soon centered on habitat management since early attempts to pen-raise grouse, unlike pheasants, were unsuccessful. In fact, many species of grouse are difficult to raise in captivity given their unique diet and love of seclusion. I recall touring a government-owned game farm in West Germany where biologists were attempting to raise capercaillie for reintroduction into the Black

Forest. Capers are the world's largest grouse and are highly sensitive to humans—perhaps because they've seen their kindred trapped, clubbed, and blasted to virtual oblivion throughout much of the European continent. In order to keep the birds from flying into posts or the top of the pens and injuring themselves, biologists stretched dark tarps across the enclosures to keep the birds under the low-light conditions similar to what they would experience in the mature forests they inhabit in the wild.

Although the American ruffed grouse wasn't in the kind of precarious position the caper was, U.S. hunters responded to the need to improve ruffed grouse habitats across the bird's range. Today, the organization has over 20,000 members in some 110 chapters across the United States and Canada.

In addition to financing research on ways to more efficiently manage for grouse, the society sponsors educational programs in a grassroots effort to teach private landowners better methods of manipulating their forests for the benefit of wildlife. In states such as Vermont, Connecticut, Massachusetts, Maryland, and Ohio, the society has enlisted the technical support of state university cooperative extension services. The program has been dubbed "COVERTS" and educates key landowners in grouse and woodcock management. Once timber management is underway, their properties are established as demonstration areas where other landowners can witness, firsthand, the habitat improvement in progress. It's hoped that this will spur other nearby landowners to implement the same management schemes.

The society works with additional groups to sponsor habitat improvement projects and advanced vocational training for wildlife professionals and forest managers. Moreover, RGS field staff members—all of whom are professional wildlife biologists or foresters—offer their technical expertise free of charge to landowners who want to improve habitat for grouse and woodcock.

## FUNDING AND MEMBERSHIP

The pipeline of funding necessary to keep these programs working comes from a variety of sources ranging from in-house projects such as merchandise sales to the Sportsmen's Banquet Program—which alone accounts for over two-thirds of the Ruffed Grouse Society's annual funding. In 1987, ninety-two banquets produced net proceeds of $865,000—nearly $10,000 per banquet. The society also receives money from grants and donations. When outside sources provide matching funds to donations made by RGS, the society's original funding serves as a catalyst to double and even triple the amount of money raised for any given project.

The original newsletter started by the organization's founders grew to become *The Drummer,* a tabloid newspaper with a variety of article topics including hunting, gun dogs, and nature. *The Drummer* in 1990 gave way to a full-color magazine titled *RGS.*

In many respects, the Ruffed Grouse Society is to the woodlands what Ducks Unlimited is to wetlands. Not only do both organizations provide sportsmen and sportswomen the opportunity to assist wildlife, but, perhaps as important, they serve as vehicles for making your statement about the hunter's role in North American wildlife conservation. The next time you leave your favorite covert, pointer at heel and a satisfying heft in your game bag, turn for a moment and look back, studying carefully the smells, sounds, and moods of the hunt. Then, and only then, try to place a dollar value on the last few hours spent afield.

Membership in The Ruffed Grouse Society includes subscription to *RGS* magazine; annual dues are $20. To join, write The Ruffed Grouse Society at 1400 Lee Drive, Coraopolis, Pennsylvania 15108. Lists of technical and popular publications are also available upon request.

# A Grouse Hunter's Closet

*To the sporting gentleman who spends more dollars on the latest in outdoor garb than he spends minutes in the woods, a ruffed grouse is something to be discussed in reverent tones.*

—David Michael Duffey, *Bird Hunting Tactics*

# A Grouse Hunter's Closet

There was a time in my life—when I began my journey into hunterdom—that I would come home from school and throw on a pair of sneakers, grab the hand-me-down Remington, and unleash my setter before traipsing off to a nearby marsh for an evening of pheasant hunting. Growing up in a relatively poor rural community had its advantages, namely that school jeans could also be worn pheasant hunting.

After two hours of setter chasing in a swamp filled with cattails, canary grass, and pheasants, I would return home soaked to my crotch. No matter, though; it was routine. I got back home while my father—who worked nights—slept and before my mother returned home from work. I peeled off the wet pants and soaked sneakers and threw them both in the clothes drier so they'd be ready for the next school day and subsequent pheasant hunt. My mother was endlessly puzzled by the amount of weed seeds left in the drier's lint trap.

Getting wet and cold seemed a natural requisite for bird hunting in my part of the world, and I always thought it little trouble compared to what an unlucky pheasant or grouse went through. It was during a solo hunt to what had become my favorite late season haunt, however, that I discovered a new degree of wet and cold and the routine lost favor with me.

A small island in the midst of the Yahara River—actually it was more of a creek than a river—was a little-known sanctuary for grouse that had been flushed from the surrounding woodlot. It was the classic "hotspot" or "bonanza" as the pedestrian outdoor tabloids of the day would have described it. It was the kind of place that frequently exists in the minds of outdoor writers but seldom in reality—at least not in my reality.

Hunters rarely if ever waded across the waist-deep moat provided by the river to discover what might await them on the island. The only reasonable time to access the island was during the late winter months when even the current of the stream succumbed to the numbing cold. A thick layer of ice turned the once inaccessible hideout to a hunter's dream by allowing anyone to trek to the covert. Though the island never housed scores of birds, almost always two or three ruffs and occasionally a rooster awaited me as I made my way across the ice.

One late January afternoon I decided to hike the necessary two miles from home to get to the island. The preceding three days had been unusually warm, and winter had until then succeeded in confining me indoors. As always with my late season hunting endeavors, I wore my school jeans, leather work boots, and a heavy parka. The hunt progressed perfectly until I tried to traverse the ice surrounding the island. Midway across—neither one-quarter nor two-thirds, but halfway—I went thrashing through the ice. I hit bottom just as my belly button submerged. With the butt of the Remington I broke a channel back to the bank.

The two-mile hike back home—warm home—was a test of endurance. My denim jeans quickly froze in the 20-degree temperatures, and the gusty winds compounded my misery. I didn't know anything about hypothermia at the time, but I knew I was cold. Damn cold. My leather boots did little more than hold frigid water and ice around my toes, and I could barely pry them from my feet when I returned home.

As a result of that incident, I have become something of a connoisseur of quality hunting apparel. Part of my job includes periodic testing of huntingwear: What works? What doesn't? Here, then, is a look inside my hunting closet of today and tomorrow.

**Boots:** The problem with good boots these days is that they cost as much as a cheap shotgun. My last pair, for instance, cost more than my first setter pup. And, of course, the dog promptly chewed the tongues out of both new boots.

The value of good boots, however, is only fully understood when a hunter wears poor quality boots. What makes a good boot? Several factors: comfort, long-lasting construction, design, and material. Much of my grouse hunting involves hiking through shallow water at some point, so I've grown fond of rubber boots. No matter how much waterproofing and how thick the Gore-Tex, leather boots simply do not endure in water as long as rubber boots.

For grouse hunting in any terrain, a boot must be lightweight. Leather, of course, has an advantage over rubber in this category. There are scores of good leather boots on the market that will serve well while hunting dry-country grouse. The best leather boots have good soles—most often that means Vibram soles. A thin Gore-Tex lining helps to keep your feet dry no matter what the conditions. Feet perspire heavily throughout a typical upland bird hunt, so you'll be more comfortable if you keep moisture off your skin, and Gore-Tex is just the material to do that.

**Brush Pants:** I remember marveling at the service I received from my first pair of brush pants. Those youthful years wearing denim jeans through blackberry and prickly ash are something of a painful memory. But I'm all the more appreciative of brush pants because of it. The ultimate goal of brush pants should be to allow you to hunt from grouse to grouse without losing any blood. Lightweight pants are comfortable for early season temperatures, but most offer little protection from heavy thorns. This is where chaps can be useful. Heavy chaps shield against thorns while allowing an open backside for plenty of ventilation.

There are numerous heavy nylon-faced pants available. The mark of quality here, in my opinion, can be seen in the stitching. I've seen the nylon facing of brush pants literally rip off under what I would consider normal grouse-hunting conditions. Check the seams carefully before opening your wallet to buy a pair of brush pants.

Zippers are another component to which I pay close attention. It's been my experience that those made of nylon not only outlast metal zippers, but also function better. Here again, check the stitching around the zippers to get an idea of the overall construction quality of the whole garment.

**Vests:** Who doesn't own a favorite vest? Why is it your favorite? There are many well-designed vests in the world, but my favorite has leather shell loops. The reason I'm so fond of leather shell loops is that I detest elastic loops. I've lost pounds of shells because of weakened elastic shell loops. Moreover, they shred at the first brush with blackberry, prickly ash, and other thorny habitats. I have passed up many otherwise well-designed vests and hunting jackets because they were made with elastic shell loops. In fact, I prefer simple pockets to elastic loops.

The value of vests over jackets is the mobility afforded the shooter. I often choose to wear a vest even during cold weather, opting to add another shirt instead of a jacket. Brown or camouflaged vests can be safely worn if a hunter wears an orange long-sleeved shirt under the vest.

**Jackets:** Grouse hunting seasons throughout much of the bird's range extend into January and even February, so inevitably a hunter needs a functional shooting jacket. Oiled-cotton coats from England have become increasingly popular among American shooters, but I am aware of none that sport bright colors.

Ease of shooting motion is critical with any shooting jacket. Comfortable design and fit are paramount. Any hitch in your shooting motion often results in an improper gun mount—a decided handicap when shotgunning. If you purchase your gear from a sporting-goods store, try on the jacket and walk over to the gun counter and ask to see one of their guns off the rack that is the same as, or similar to, the one you hunt with. Practice shouldering the gun several times to get the feel of the required motion needed for a perfect shoulder and cheek fit.

**Hats, Gloves, and Glasses:** Wear all three. There are many styles of hats, so find a comfortable one colored blaze orange and use it afield. In most of my favorite grouse haunts, gloves lean closer to necessity than luxury. They're certainly needed in cold weather, but leather shooting gloves also provide protection against the thorns and thistles so often a part of productive grouse habitat. Shooting glasses not only protect your eyes from stray BBs, but also may be vision-savers should a thorn branch snap into your face as you hunt. Many are offered in optic-yellow and allow improved vision under low-light conditions. Shooters with vision prescriptions can normally order shooting glasses through their optometrists.

---

### A PLEA FOR ORANGE

Having been shot once while afield, I can attest to the value of wearing blaze orange. Though I didn't sustain any lasting physical injuries, I will not soon forget the experience. Looking down the open end of a gun barrel was sobering, but hearing a shell discharge and feeling BBs pop all over my chest was terrifying. I'm seldom comfortable hunting with those who don't wear at least some article of orange clothing.

Hunting clothes that don't display any orange should have warning labels on them: "Wearing this garment is hazardous to your health—especially if worn while hunting with others." Each time I see grouse hunters enter the woods wearing brown or camouflaged clothing, I'm reminded of the coyote who repeatedly uses unsafe gadgets to try to catch the roadrunner: "This product is guaranteed for the life of the user." Enough said.

# Dogs to Fit a Covert

*Each grouse casts its spell on the sport, and the dog and the gunner reflect this. Certain coverts are remembered, not for great numbers of birds but for a particular grouse and a moment of splendor.*

—George Bird Evans, "The Thorns"

# Dogs to Fit a Covert

**A** great grouse dog, first and foremost, must have a sense of humor. A bird dog that is able to point a grouse and act unfazed when I miss will make great strides in befriending me for life. Aside from drive, a keen nose, and an ability to recognize prime cover, the best grouse dogs I've ever hunted with had the good sense not to stare at me after I missed.

Grouse hunters since time immemorial have lobbied heartily for one breed or another. Some favor the style of the setter; others esteem the no-nonsense approach of the continental breeds; still others prefer the efficiency of the pointer; and some swear by their old Lab that "never gets out of range."

Before reviewing a list of popular breeds used for grouse hunting, it's important first to understand that there are three common types of bird dogs: pointers, flushers, and retrievers. Pointing dogs harbor a natural instinct that tells them to stop and point birds when they locate bird scent. Ideally, they will hold this point at least long enough for the hunter to walk past the dog, flush, and possibly even shoot the birds. Flushers, however, merely vacuum nearby cover until they spook a bird to flight. In order for flushers to be assets for hunters, the dogs must flush birds within shooting range. Lastly, retrievers act as flushing dogs in the field and are often especially adept at finding downed birds, hence the reason they are grouped as retrievers.

As a hell-bent, ever-loving setter devotee, I am tempted to espouse the virtues of this grand breed, but to do so would be a mistake. The fact is, I have grown fond of these white pooches over the years, but no more fond than a good friend of mine is of his Labrador retriever or another friend is of his German shorthairs. Each, for his own reasons, has chosen his own favorite breed. Moreover, I don't ascribe to the one-best-breed-of-dog theory when it comes to grouse dogs.

A better way to select the right dog for you is to carefully examine your own hunting style. It is you, after all, who will be hunting with the dog, not a kennel owner who happens to have a certain breed in surplus. Do you poke along through the coverts, or do you prefer a quick pace to cover as much ground as possible? Do you have the time necessary to develop a pointing dog? Will you be using the dog to hunt other game birds? These are but a few questions grouse hunters need to ask themselves before mortgaging their next decade of bird hunting.

## CONSIDERING BIRD DOGS BY BREED

Although I've never been fond of relying on "general" breed characteristics as a way of matching hunter with dog, such consideration does offer the hunter a guideline with which to work. This approach is far too superficial, however, and conventional wisdom rightly holds that a hunter should investigate a pup's immediate ancestors and their hunting habits before committing to purchase the pup. By so doing, you reduce your chance of selecting a dog that will not suit your needs.

With that caution, let me offer a general review of the commonly exhibited traits of some of the popular breeds. First, let's examine the continental or versatile hunting breeds—German shorthaired pointers, vizslas, Drahthaars, and the like—to see if they may be a breed in your future.

I have hunted grouse behind all three of these breeds and have enjoyed considerable success, thank you. There's nothing flashy about the way these dogs go about a grouse hunt, but, for the most part, they are reliable hunters with a blue-collar, workmanlike approach to game. They also tend to be more consistent retrievers than other breeds that work faster, running past downed game. This same ground-tracking tendency, however, can get these dogs into trouble if they haven't had much experience locating skittish grouse. A dog that follows ground scent—as opposed to the scent emanating directly from the bird—will occasionally fail to recognize how close it has come to a grouse until it is too late and the bird has escaped to friendlier habitat. If you're not bothered by the proposition of shooting at grouse that are not flushed from under point, then a plodding dog may offer no disadvantage as it typically works close enough to provide shooting at birds it bumps or flushes.

In stark contrast to the continental breeds is the pointer, formerly known as the English pointer. These dogs—or robo-dogs—are God's way of striking fear in quail. Anyone who has ever watched a whip-tailed pointer blow through a quail plantation has seen the epitome of a bird-finding machine. The problem for most grouse hunters is twofold. First, pointers quite often range much too far to be effective in the close confines of an alder thicket where visibility can be fifteen feet or less. Even a slow pointer can cover fifteen feet in a tail-wag. Second, these strong-willed dogs have been known to break their owners before the inverse occurs. For pure bird-finding ability, however, the pointer has no equal, and dogs that can be controlled within whistle distance have the potential to be truly great pointers.

The English setter falls somewhere between the continentals and the pointer in both the way it ranges and the way it finds birds. It is easy to fall in love with the stylish gait and classic points associated with setters. This breed generally ranges farther than the continentals but closer than pointers, though I've had setters that could run a close footrace with almost any pointer—or quarter horse, for that matter. Pointers and setters both use their noses as wind gauges, ideally feathering into the breeze with nose skyward, searching for bird scent. The long hair of the setter makes it an appealing choice for northern grouse hunting, where pointers are more likely to be bothered by cold temperatures and sharp briars.

Another popular breed with northern grouse hunters is the Brittany spaniel. The Brittany has what many consider the optimal range for grouse hunting—commonly thirty to sixty yards. Like the continental breeds, the Britt is a close-working woodsmith that likes its grouse scent hot and is a popular pointer among grouse hunters. These dogs can range from the small, fox-muzzled French variety to the big-boned, square-headed dogs that resemble English setters in body conformation.

A breed that has gained prominence throughout the last decade is the Gordon setter. Though I have never hunted behind a Gordon, I have seen several compete in field trials designed for hunting dogs. I cannot think of a breed that has a more loyal following than the Gordon, the other breeds be damned! As with the English setter, there are two distinct divisions of Gordon: the smaller field strain and the large-bodied bench or show setters. Gordon setters are stunningly handsome dogs that their owners will attest are as effective in the field as they are attractive in the show ring.

Flushing breeds commonly used to hunt grouse include a wide assortment from spaniels to Labs. Any close-working flushing dog that can find downed grouse will be an asset in the uplands. In a Wisconsin study conducted at the Sandhill Experimental Wildlife Area, more than 60 percent of the grouse hunters on the property hunted with dogs, and they accounted for more than 80 percent of the birds harvested.

## DEFINING GREATNESS

Great grouse dogs are the precious gems of a grouse hunter's life, coveted by those who long for one memorable pointer in their lives. These dogs must have a superb nose in order to locate grouse from a great distance, for grouse won't stand to be crowded. The best grouse dogs possess an innate sense that tells them when they have approached close enough to the bird. It's as if dog and bird are two positively charged ions, able to come only so close before one forces the other away.

The greatness of a grouse dog is measured in consistency. My oldest setter is an adequate grouse dog but, I must admit, will not reach the Grouse Dogs' Hall of Fame. I fear he may have been corrupted during his early years as a pheasant addict. He has provided the single greatest one-day performance I have ever witnessed in the aspen, but the half of his brain used for grouse hunting is prone to suddenly surrender to the other half that controls pheasant-hunting synapses. The result is a dog that is about 60 percent pointer and 40 percent flusher. From the plethora of different grouse dogs I've hunted with, that point-to-flush ratio is on a par with what some of the better ones demonstrate. The simple fact remains that there is much to grouse that will always be a mystery—even to the best grouse dogs.

A pointer that is trained to be steady to wing and shot, not breaking when the bird erupts and the hunter shoots, and obedient to stop-to-flush, however, is a decidedly more effective assistant in the uplands. I wish I could say that is a lesson learned from having trained a dog to such an end, but, I'm afraid, I arrived at this opinion after having owned dogs who possess neither degree of training. I have, happily, shared hunts with dogs who are steady to wing and shot, and I can assure skeptics that it is a most valuable skill when pursuing grouse and woodcock. Since grouse are a wholly paranoid bird, a dog that is in control at all times will reduce your chances of spooking an entire family of grouse following a shot at one bird. Many dogs are wont to sprint after the bird they are pointing when it flushes, thereby spooking most nearby birds.

The debate between hunters who favor a pointer steady to wing and shot and those who merely think the dog should remain staunch until the point of flush is as old as the choke collar. The classic argument goes something like this: "I want a dog that gets after a bird the moment it's flushed so that the dog can be in position

Hunter harvests are carefully monitored as part of the research being conducted on the Sandhill Wildlife Area in central Wisconsin. (*Photo © by Dave Otto*)

Surveys of grouse hunters indicate that dogs increase a hunter's chance of encountering ruffs dramatically. Hunter check stations are also used to confirm this and other information about hunter impact on the birds. (*Photo © by John Kubisiak*)

Increasing pressure on small public hunting areas has led some biologists to rethink traditional beliefs about the effect of human hunting on grouse populations. (*Photo © by Chris Dorsey*)

Bag limits on grouse are as liberal today as they have been at any time in history since the days of market hunting. (*Photo © by Tom Martinson*)

Spring drumming counts are used to gauge the rise and fall of grouse populations. Such surveys provide an index by which biologists project the numbers of grouse that survived the winter. (*Photo* © *by Tom Martinson*)

Ravens contribute to grouse mortality by occasionally raiding nests. (*Photo © by Tom Martinson*)

The future. Understanding more about the biology of grouse and their habitat requirements is an ongoing focus of the Ruffed Grouse Society. (*Photo* © *by John Kubisiak*)

This Union Town, Pennsylvania, Ruffed Grouse Society Banquet is just one of scores of such events that are designed to raise funds for RGS. In 1987, ninety-two banquets produced net proceeds of $865,000. (*Photo © by Paul Carson*)

Remington's line of hunting clothes includes this heavy jacket that is designed especially for cool-weather outings. (*Photo* © *by Chris Dorsey*)

The author used Cabela's Brittany boots on a spruce and ruffed grouse hunt in Manitoba. The boot's Vibram sole is largely responsible for its comfort. (*Photo © by Chris Dorsey*)

By carefully considering your needs—not wants—you can save money be eliminating unnecessary purchases. (*Photo © by Chris Dorsey*)

This Dunn's vest is geared for early-season hunting. Its leather shell loops are vastly superior to elastic loops found in other jackets and vests. (*Photo © by Chris Dorsey*)

You've probably seen the advertisements used to market this Filson vest. They depict a quote from a hunter who has used this vest, "every year for the past 53 years." (*Photo courtesy Filson Company*)

Wet aspen and alder swamps in the Great Lakes make the LaCrosse Rubber Hikers (*left*) an appropriate choice for grouse hunters, while the Russell Bird Shooter Boots are classics for upland hunting. (*Photo © by Chris Dorsey*)

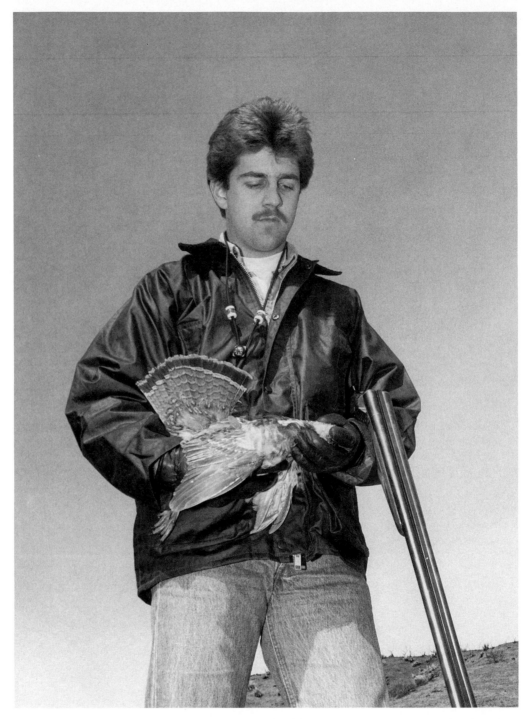

Oiled cotton clothes imported from England have gained considerable favor with American wingshots in recent years. This Uplander jacket from Lewis Creek offers features most grouse hunters want. (*Photo © by Dave Hetzler*)

The L.L. Bean vest and Bob Allen pants are just two products in a long line of hunting clothes made by both American firms. (*Photo* © *by Chuck Petrie*)

Columbia Sportswear's Grouse Parka and Pants were designed to handle the tough country associated with grouse hunting. The jacket's blaze orange color makes it an ideal garment when hunting with others. (*Photo © by Chuck Petrie*)

to make the retrieve as soon as possible, before the bird has a chance to run."

Those who favor a steady-to-wing-and-shot pointer—myself included—counter: "A dog steady to wing and shot will seldom lose any additional birds because of a delayed retrieve on a downed grouse and is a far more pleasant companion afield for the simple fact that it is always under the coaching of its owner instead of running after a bird that may or may not be hit."

A steady-to-wing-and-shot pointer can be worth its weight in tailfeathers when the northern flights of woodcock descend into your favorite coverts. I'll forever remember one morning in 1978 when what seemed to be all of Canada's woodcock rode the head winds of an Alberta clipper and landed on a small, alder-strewn island in the midst of a cattail swamp. The island, roughly four acres, was surrounded by superb pheasant habitat. Few people ever made it to the island because sloshing over required hip boots to traverse the thigh-deep moat surrounding the treasured island. By the time the water froze and hunters could trek to the holding, the woodcock were already wintering in Louisiana as migrants or as Cajun entrées.

While the island had always been a favorite recluse where vagabond woodcock could stow away, this morning was unlike any I'd seen. It was a mecca for the birds; I lost count of the flushes—somewhere over fifty. Thor pointed his first bird ten feet onto the island. I flushed the bird and shot twice, missing on both accounts. He immediately left point and proceeded to flush a virtually endless stream of woodcock that continued to circle the island like ducks over decoys. With an overpowering dose of woodcock scent behind every alder stem, the young dog was unable to control his urge to chase the birds. What should have been an easy limit of timberdoodles turned into a frustrating game of setter tag. The experience is perhaps as vivid in Thor's mind as it is in mine. If only he had possessed the discipline of a five-year-old instead of his yearling vigor.

But in many ways, woodcock are a pointing dog's best friend. They are notoriously tight-sitting birds that will often let a pointer approach within sneezing distance. I have seen woodcock fly from underfoot as if taking a direct course to the next state south, and I've also seen them flush and land twenty feet away. Their behavior is unpredictable at best. I often think it must be entirely confusing for a pointing dog that is trying to point both grouse and woodcock in the same covert. While woodcock are tolerant of nearby dog bells, grouse, on the other hand, need a wide berth or they'll flush prematurely.

Such are the dilemmas an upland dog must face each time it endeavors to please its owner—now if only the one with the gun wouldn't miss.

# A Truly Great Grouse Dog?

The dog knows what is grouseward better than you do. You will do well to follow him closely, reading from the cock of his ears the story the breeze is telling.
— Aldo Leopold, *A Sand County Almanac*

# A Truly Great Grouse Dog?

There are those who hunt grouse without dogs and, I must add, kill plenty of birds. But sometimes the question of whether a dog will increase your daily bag of grouse is not so much a matter of function, but rather of purpose. A hunter who regards a dog merely as equipment to use in killing birds will treat that dog no differently than a shotgun or pair of boots. Its passing soon will be forgotten like the fate of an auctioned head of livestock.

My closest grouse-hunting friends appreciate fine guns, enjoy good companionship, but love their dogs. To them, even a poor day afield with a pointer is better than the best hunt without a dog. Grouse hunting without a dog is an incomplete experience. You might even take more grouse alone, but what of the value of an eager tail-wag, the music of dog bells, a lick on the cheek? How utterly dull life must be for those who will never see the real purpose of a bird dog.

A line from the contributor's guide to *Gun Dog* magazine aptly describes my association with grouse dogs and the men who own them: "If the typical subscriber was given the opportunity to hunt the best covert or marsh in North America, but under the condition that he could take either his gun or his dog, not both, he'd choose his dog."

Here, then, are five such men. They are, simply, the best at what they do. Charley Dickey, David Michael Duffey, John Falk, Bill Tarrant, and Charles Waterman are not part of the who's who of American dog writers, they *are* the who's who. What makes them so, you ask? A trip through their prose and you will discover a mirror reflecting your experiences, your dogs—past, present, and future. Their insight into dogs and hunters offers more than the pedantic how-to drivel so often pitched to the average reader.

I posed this question to each of them: What makes a truly great grouse dog? What follows are their unique and sage answers, drawn from decades of personal experience with the comical and sometimes magnificent creature known as the grouse dog.

## CHARLEY DICKEY: A RELIABLE GROUSE DOG?

*Prior to his career in writing, Dickey spent twenty-two years divided among the Tennessee Conservation Department, Olin's Winchester-Western Division, the Sportsman's Service Bureau, and as a director of the National Shooting Sports Foundation. His works have appeared in a variety of magazines including* Field & Stream, Esquire, Sports Afield, Playboy, Outdoor Life, True, Argosy, *and many others. He is also a monthly columnist in* Petersen's Hunting *magazine and has authored eight books. Two of the best books are still in print:* Opening Shots and Parting Lines *and* Movin' Along with Charley Dickey.

The ruffed grouse is not a stable, dependable bird, especially in its tolerance for pointing dogs. Under one set of circumstances, the bird will squat tightly and hold under the hot breath of a pointer. Under identical circumstances, but five minutes later, the ruff wouldn't hold in a steel trap.

The behavior of a grouse is unpredictable because the bird itself doesn't know until the last instant if it will hold, walk, run, or fly, or a combination of all four. Since the hunter can't count on a trustworthy bird, he needs a reliable dog.

The genes and training of the dog should take into account what the dog will encounter in the field. The breed does not matter.

Since grouse are spooky about holding, the pointing breed should have a keen nose. The further away a grouse is pointed, the more likely it is to be in the vicinity when the hunter arrives with a shotgun.

The ideal dog methodically quarters the cover directly in front of hunters. Even if the dog doesn't make an error, a grouse may flush on its own. Hopefully it will be close enough for the hunters to get off a shot before the bird is out of range or disappears in dense cover.

It is important that the dog is convinced that its owner knows a little about grouse hunting. A lot of time is wasted, and no birds killed, when the dog hunts one area and the hunter another.

The dog should also be unflappable. The dog may perfectly indicate a holding grouse without moving a muscle or even breathing loudly. The grouse may hold until the gunner is almost in range. Then it will flush without provocation. The frustrated hunter blames the dog, who was flawless, and the dog is called bad names or worse. Emotional complexes kill more grouse dogs than old age.

For hunting any species of game birds with pointing dogs, the most important command for the dog to learn is "Whoa!" It's doubly important for dogs with ambition to make a reputation as grouse dogs, for a dog that strays too far will spook birds out of sight. A lot of dogs know the command but are not good at practicing it when put down in a grouse woods.

As for putting grouse in the bag, the best ruff dogs I've ever seen afield were a brace of scrawny white setters in the mountains of western North Carolina. Most of the terrain was straight up or straight down. The hunters were always out of breath. If the dogs pointed seventy-five yards away, it might take fifteen minutes to rappel within fifty yards. By the time you got within flushing range, the grouse might have departed thirty minutes earlier.

The owner taught his dogs to whoa on command, to come to a grinding halt at the first indication they were making game. If a dog's head went high to catch more wind, or a dog's tail began to wag faster, the owner yelled, "Whoa!" That would give us a chance to close up on the dogs.

Then he'd send the dogs on to trail the bird, with us right on their heels. It didn't matter if the bird walked, ran, or flushed. Whenever it decided to fly, we'd be in range for a shot or two. We got a lot of scratches and skint knees staying on those setters' butts, but we also bagged a lot of ruffs. It was sort of a bonus when we got two guns concentrated for a shot over a point.

## DAVID MICHAEL DUFFEY: ICONOCLASTIC GROUSE DOGS

*Although he currently resides in northeastern Mississippi, David Michael Duffey grew up and spent most of his life in Wisconsin's ruffed grouse covers. A self-professed "hunter and dog trainer who happens to write," Duffey has been at it for almost fifty years. He's penned eight books on gun dog training and hunting, four of them—* Hunting Dog Know How, Bird Hunting Tactics, Expert Advice on Gun Dog Training, *and* How to Train Your Best Friend—*are still in print. He's currently gun dog editor with Petersen's* Hunting *and writes columns for* Gun Dog, Wing & Shot, *and* Hunting Retriever *magazines. He spent twenty-three years as hunting dogs editor with* Outdoor Life *and has contributed to scores of encyclopedias and anthologies about hunting dogs. He has probably written more about hunting dogs than any writer, past or present.*

When seeking a dog to do you proud while hunting ruffed grouse, should someone tell you he owns or knows of "a real good grouse and woodcock dog"—unless he's referring to a spaniel or retriever, both flushing dogs—refrain from reaching for your wallet.

Traditionally, grouse dogs to remember come from the ranks of the pointing breeds. English setters with "part grouse blood" are considered classics. Poke-around Brittanys are also practical for anyone interested in shooting over points or stops-to-flush following minimal training. Since the covers frequented by the two bird species overlap, dogs commonly get to work both ruffed grouse and woodcock.

However, serious hunters recognize that, if separated, a good "woodcock dog" and a good "grouse dog" differ greatly. So when describing their pointers, hunters prefer to lump them as "grouse and woodcock dogs," thereby expiating some pretty sorry performances on grouse with some classy work on woodcock.

No dog that handles ruffed grouse well will have any trouble doing the same to woodcock. But a heap of woodcock whizbangs are, at best, mediocre to fair in coping with ruffs.

Rarely is that the case when the flushing breeds are developed as genuine grouse and woodcock hunters. Expect spaniels and retrievers to do well on both partridge and timberdoodles.

So I offer the iconoclastic suggestion that at least 75 percent of the brush-busters and bog-sloggers who follow dogs in the uplands will get more, and sometimes better, shooting by partnering up with a pretty ordinary spaniel or retriever than they will by using any but an outstanding individual from among the pointing breeds.

Old *Bonasa umbellus* is tough for any pointing dog to master. So, most really good ruffed grouse specialists of traditional choice take years to develop and seldom are sold. For the hunter thrilled more by stylishly staunch points than by the gunning aspect of the hunt, of course, setters, pointers, Brittanys, or continental breeds are the only routes to go.

Large numbers of much-appreciated, highly praised grouse dogs of pointing persuasion hunt within or just beyond shotgun range. If sportsmen need "naturally" short-ranging pointing dogs or manage to restrict the range of more ebullient individuals, they will have less trouble finding a "natural" or training to quarter when buying a spaniel or retriever pup.

Essentially, about the only thing that will seriously mar the effectiveness of a hunting spaniel or retriever is wild running, out-of-range flushing.

Seeking game within gun range is the flushing dog's equivalent of the pointing dog's staunchness once pinpointed game scent halts him. As a practical matter, few hunters require manners beyond that, in either flushers or pointers. But all hunters want their grouse dogs to be fetchers.

When it comes to recovering downed game, run-of-the-mill spaniels and retrievers will beat all but the unusual pointing breed representative. In thick grouse cover, more important than their innate marking superiority is the spaniel and retriever inclination and willingness to put their noses down and seek out any type or trace of scent. Pointers, on the other hand, are usually more apt and eager to seek fresh quarry.

Having shot ruffed grouse (and woodcock) over just about any gun dog breed you can name, while I lean toward a good pointer or setter as a personal preference, I believe spaniels and retrievers have put more birds in my game vest.

So it might be worthwhile for a lot of hunters to buck tradition and give a springer spaniel or a Labrador retriever (or American water, Boykin, and English working cocker spaniels, or Chesapeake and golden retrievers) a chance to prove how well they're capable of doing in the grouse thickets and woodcock runs.

## JOHN R. FALK: THE PERFECT DOG

*Although Johnny Falk's full-time occupation is public relations manager of Olin Corporation's Winchester Division, he also serves as gun dog editor for* Shooting Sportsman *magazine and is the author of three books:* The Young Sportsman's Guide to Dogs, The Practical Hunter's Dog Book, *and* The Complete Guide to Bird Dog Training. *His articles have appeared in a wide assortment of magazines, including* Field & Stream, Sports Afield, American Sportsman, Guns & Hunting, *and many others.*

Aah, the perfect grouse dog! A meditation to stir even the most jaded imagination. Asking to define such perfection, though, presumes its existence, and the embodiment of perfection looms far more challenging to find than merely framing a plausible description. Still, wouldn't the perfect grouse dog necessarily have to be virtually synonymous with the perfect grouse, still another candidate for definition? Can there be one without the other? I wonder.

Consider, for a moment, such a quarry: a perfect grouse. No tenant of antagonistic alders, harrowing hawthorns, or clawing conifers, this bird. A habitué only of coverts lightly treed, on slopes gently angled for easy walking, it would always lie tight at approach of dog and gun. Its flush, obligingly, would eschew the sudden, startling thunder of wings for a more considerate ascent on whisper-soft pinions.

Shedding its vexatious behavior in exchange for absolute predictability, it would seek escape in straight-line, level flight, never twisting, dodging, diving to sideslip a string of No. 7½ shot. It would be, in short, a true gentleman, a real lady . . . indeed, a perfect grouse. Sadly, though, to the legions of devoted followers who know and cherish this creature, it would also be . . . a perfect stranger. And, Lord, who among us would trade a respected friend for a perfect stranger?

So, just as the consummate grouse does not, cannot, exist, neither does its counter-part canine. But happily, good, even occasionally great, grouse dogs do.

While some grouse sages steer carefully around committing to one breed or even one type of dog for hunting *Bonasa umbellus*, I openly admit to unabashed partiality. For my grouse hunting only a pointing dog need apply, and if he/she is not an English setter, then he/she will have to wait in line.

How do I rate a first-class grouse-hunting setter? Highest priority is the quality "learnability," the intelligence and capacity truly to absorb and profit from experience. A dog that goes along from season to season changing little in approach to the quarry, seldom adjusting speed and range to cover conditions, can never hope for greatness or even improved performance. But the dog that, in its third or fourth season, begins to stand fast at strong grouse scent instead of taking that extra step or two closer that too often bumped birds last year is the dog I want.

My choice dog must have a good, maybe extra-good, nose to start with, and increasingly bolster its and my confidence in it. Equally important, while seeking our quarry, its and mine, the dog must work its ground sensibly, selecting likely objectives while avoiding or not dawdling over unpromising stretches. Since the dog will be hunting with and for me—and I won't be the one wearing a bell—I expect my companion to check in frequently and to handle kindly, with a minimum of direction.

Most of these qualities I will have no part in infusing in my dog; they will be there from the start, bequeathed by proven-in-the-field ancestors. What I must contribute is an ideal environment in which those attributes can be nurtured to peak promise. And that prescription includes patience, prudent guidance, and frequent opportunities to hunt in areas of grouse abundance. For without grouse, lots and lots of grouse, a great grouse dog can never be.

## BILL TARRANT: PUTTING THE BIRD INTO DOGS

*Currently gun dog editor for* Field & Stream, *Bill Tarrant has won twenty-three national writing awards since 1977. He's a former professor of journalism at Wichita State University and has authored four books:* Best Way to Train Your Gun Dog *(currently in its eighteenth printing),* Hey Pup, Fetch It Up!, Bill Tarrant's Gun Dog Book, *and* Tarrant Trains Gun Dogs. *The former mayor of Wichita, Kansas, he now resides in Sedona, Arizona, where he continues to train dogs and hunt birds.*

Know this about bird dogs. Bird is half the name, the first half—and all the game. Yet we continually slight birds in our training programs because they represent work, we don't know how to handle them, and we want to think we can train a dog without them. Ha! Impossible! Especially for the grouse hunter. Here's why.

What bird is spookier and testier than the ruffed grouse? None. And the reason we see so much poor dog work on grouse is because Pup crowds the cone of scent emanating from the bird. But a dog properly trained with tons of birds can slam on point and apply power quite distant, forcing the grouse to set for the gun.

For a dog to honor the outermost edge of a scent cone, it must be taken directly from playful puppyhood to controlled bird contacts. This means the handler check-cords Pup to the fringe of the scent cone of a planted bird and whoas the dog, totally, immediately. Then silently and cautiously the handler comes hand over hand down the cord until he's beside the dog. Now he crouches, places the knee next to Pup to the ground, circles Pup's waist with the near arm, bends the far knee and plants that foot solid, then grasps Pup's collar with the far hand. Pup can't bolt, rear back, jump to side, or duck inside. Pup's anchored. Now the bird boy circles the area (far out) and comes in on the planted and hobbled bird. He lifts the bird and gives a feather dance, hurrahing, letting the bird fly on its cord, making that bird the most exciting thing Pup has ever seen. Then the bird is launched, the handler grasping Pup, as Pup watches the bird down to later relocate or fetch deadfall.

This session is repeated until Pup slams the breaks at the first whiff of a scent cone. Now you've got a grouse dog in the making. Let Delmar Smith of Edmond, Oklahoma, proponent of "distant whoa," explain. Delmar's a professional trainer whose dogs have won ten national Brittany championships.

Delmar was running in a field trial outside Boston and called point on a grouse. The judge rode up and told Delmar, "Release your dog to go on. That'll be unproductive. If there was a grouse in there, he's gone. Grouse don't hold for a point."

Delmar asked, "Mind if I go in there and stomp around?"

Irritated, the judge replied, "All right, but it's a waste of time."

Delmar entered cover—far to the front of the pointing dog— and worked back, kicking around. Up popped the grouse. The dog won the trial, the judge telling the gallery, "In thirty years of judging, that's the only time I've ever ridden to a point on grouse and seen it flushed."

Finally, let me emphasize this truth. Don't think dogs can't transfer immediately from yard pointing a tame pigeon to field pointing a wild grouse. Consider, each summer many Dixie professionals go North to work the Canadian prairies. The birds pointed are Hungarian partridges and sharptailed grouse. Yet, immediately upon returning South for the fall field trial circuit the dogs lock on bobwhite.

So, know nothing about bird dog training but this and you'll turn out a stellar grouse dog. Nothing beats birds—and nothing except stopping Pup at the absolute edge of the scent cone.

## CHARLES WATERMAN: BASICS FIRST

*Currently on staff with six magazines, Charles Waterman began writing outdoor stories in 1934. Now seventy-six years old, he is the author of sixteen books on hunting and fishing. His hunting titles include* The Hunter's World, Hunting Upland Birds, Hunting in America, *and* Gun Dogs and Bird Guns. *He and his wife, Debie, reside in Florida during the winter but journey to Montana during the summer and fall. His widely acclaimed writings have made him the dean of American sporting writers.*

Good grouse dogs tend to be individuals. Old Mac, who often hunted in very heavy cover, would climb partway up a brushy tree and growl when a ruff surveyed him from a safe height. Old Tex barked when he pointed grouse. Such procedures are unconventional and are seldom advocated in dog-training manuals.

It happened that both of these long-gone old-timers were Brittanys, although similar habits are employed by specialists of other breeds, and it may be that English setters have produced more tall but truthful tales about American grouse pointing, having been at it longer. Grouse-hunting German shepherds should not be discounted—but, like collies, they do not tend to specialize in grouse. Regardless of breed, there are some common qualifications, possibly best expressed by a brand-new grouse hunter.

"I want a grouse dog that comes when I call him," said the novice.

At first I thought this requirement was pretty childish, but such talent covers a lot of underbrush, willows, and quaking aspen. The most important thing of all, whether the dog's a flusher or a pointer, is that it be controllable. The dog must be a close worker, of course, and that comes under "control." Of course, there is always the possibility that you might get some shots at grouse while hunting for a lost dog, but there are better ways. Old grouse dogs are almost invariably better than young grouse dogs.

I've shot most of my grouse in the West, where they aren't hunted much and still retain the stigma of "fool hen" in some places. They do sit on branches and stare at me sometimes, refusing to fly until I throw a stick, after which they tend to dive and are impossible to hit. At other times they drift off through the timber as silently as owls or roar off the ground while I am looking for them in the branches. Sometimes they walk into places so thick neither I nor my dog can follow, and they tend to stare studiously back at us. Since I have followed only two dogs that vocally announced the presence of grouse, I have invested in a variety of bells and beepers. These noisemakers, I feel, are secondary only to the gun and dog in hunting grouse.

But the single best description of a good grouse dog is "brilliantly cooperative."

# Grouse Dogs and Field Trials

*There is a certain symbiosis between hunter and bird dog, a mutually beneficial relationship which makes each a better performer in the uplands.*
　　　　　　　　　　　　—Dennis Walrod, *Grouse Hunter's Guide*

# Grouse Dogs and Field Trials

**A** dog first gets wind of a grouse. The dog begins a lashing tail-wag until the moment it points or flushes the bird. In this moment of anticipation a hunter can find much of the real value of a grouse dog. A person who hunts alone has only the instantaneous thunder of a flush to remember, while a hunter with a dog remembers the pointer's puffing cheeks, glaring eyes, and blood-tipped tail. A dog driven by old ruff may eat food, but make no mistake, it is fueled by grouse scent.

A grouse dog's enthusiasm for the game is an electric phenomenon that has a way of charging its owner. It is what makes normally sane people load up the pickup and strike off for grouse coverts in the midst of a rainstorm. These same people are part of an almost cultlike group of grouse field trialers. Each spring and fall, throughout the ruffed grouse's range, hunt clubs sponsor field trials for grouse hunters and their dogs. They are celebrations of the bird as much as they are contests for the dog.

The thought of field trials—simulated hunts to test and show the abilities of hunting dogs—for many grouse hunters is taboo; it evokes the same sort of passionate response normally reserved for crooked politicians. To reduce a grouse hunt to a contest, think some, is to change the purpose of the experience. A grouse hunt is a singular celebration in and of itself. A dog's ability to find grouse is measured individually by its owner, not by the judgment of others.

And this is why a field trial for grouse differs considerably from, say, the big-dollar dog races associated with southern quail matches. The majority of hunting-dog field trials I've attended are more a social gathering for gun dog zealots than a play-for-keeps competition. Local sporting clubs and even some of the over 110 Ruffed Grouse Society chapters across North America sponsor the events prior to the hunting season in August and September. Some trials, however, are held concurrently with the grouse and woodcock season and offer the added dimension of shooting and retrieving grouse.

The numerous state and local trials culminate each fall with the Grand National Grouse Championship, an event begun in 1939. The Grand National is held in a different location each year, and participants include many winning entries from other previous trials.

## TRIALS OF JUDGING

The Grand National may draw eighty or more grouse hunters and their pointing dogs from the United States and Canada and lasts several days. A random drawing is made to pair the dogs in what is called a brace. Each brace runs a predetermined course for roughly one hour. Dog handlers follow their pointers on foot while a pair of judges follow on horseback, making notes about each dog's performance.

Judges can be a finicky lot. In the back of even the most objective judge's mind is a tiny corner of the brain that stores what that person considers to be the characteristics of the ideal grouse dog. The best judges suppress such biases, but to be a bird hunter is to carry a certain degree of prejudice. One judge may favor the style of a setter, another the speed of a pointer. But a truly great grouse dog often transcends such hidden biases, and these are the kinds of dogs that are likely to win hunting-dog field trials.

A dog that quarters evenly through only the best grouse cover and keeps track of its owner is well on its way to endearing itself to most judges. A staunch pointer that finds several grouse with an air of confidence will be hard to beat—whether competing in a field trial or hunting your choicest coverts. Such dogs are students of many hours of yard and field training. No matter how many pigeons are shot over a developing grouse dog, there is no substitute for time afield in pursuit of ruffs.

The same is true for pheasant or quail dogs. I recall a hunting-dog trial a number of years ago in which I entered my setter who had developed a degree of sophistication when it came to finding and pointing pheasants, but as of then had no experience stalking grouse or woodcock. The trial sponsors had obtained dozens of pen-raised pheasants for the event, but part of the trial's course included a ten-to fifteen-minute stint through an alder and aspen bottom. I drew the first brace and proceeded with my exuberant young prospect, who broke out of the starting gate like a thoroughbred at the Belmont racetrack. After a couple of years of hunting sprint-happy Midwestern pheasants, my setter began performing a forty- to sixty-yard semicircle loop around each bird he faced. This tactic trapped running birds between me and the pointing setter. I received numerous compliments from hunting companions about the high degree of training it must have taken to coach the dog to perform such a loop. I freely accepted the praise without telling anyone that I had nothing to do with this particular behavior, that it was simply a learned response.

As my brace-mates and I entered the alder thicket, my setter began his loop around a woodcock. Woodcock, unlike pheasants, see little merit in trying to outrun a threat. Why, they probably suppose, would God have given us wings? The judges were dumbfounded by this peculiar loop, and in the time that it took for me to explain to them why my setter was behaving in such a manner, the other dog in the brace, a pointer, had already located the woodcock.

"That's the strangest thing I've ever seen," said one judge.

"How do you go about breaking a dog of such a habit?" asked the other.

## HOW TO ENTER GROUSE TRIALS

The *American Field* is a Chicago-based tabloid that keeps a pulse on most of the sanctioned field trials held across the country. Announcements of forthcoming gun dog events of all sorts appear in this newspaper. Annual subscription to this weekly paper is $25 and can be ordered from 542 South Dearborn Street, Chicago, Illinois 60605. In addition, contact your nearest chapter of the Ruffed Grouse Society for information about any trials they might sponsor. Many RGS chapters have separate committees whose sole purpose is to sponsor an annual or semiannual field trial. To locate your nearest RGS chapter, write: The Ruffed Grouse Society, 1400 Lee Drive, Coraopolis, Pennsylvania 15108.

# Grouse Guns

*Take the shotguns from my life and take the books that go with them. Take the paintings and the etchings and bronzed pointing setters and Labs with a proudly carried duck.*

—Gene Hill, "Our World Without Shotguns"

# Grouse Guns

**M**any similarities mark the American auto and gun industries. Both built a preponderance of heavy, bulky products while many in the market were looking for trimmed-down, sleek models. In both cases, American consumers found foreign products more to their liking. These short-barreled, lightweight shotguns, originally available from Europe and Japan, have been sorely needed in the uplands ever since the first nimrod ventured through an alder patch and was scared to the treetops by a flushing grouse. Only since the 1970s, however, have American gun manufacturers widely catered to the 2.4 million grouse hunters who hike the continent. Frank Woolner, in his 1970 work, *Grouse and Grouse Hunting,* was one of the first American writers to extol the virtues of a lightweight gun in the uplands.

## ONE CHOICE GUN

If I were stranded on a grouse-infested island and had the choice of only one gun to use to kill enough grouse to sustain myself, what specifications would I ask for in that gun? It would have a short, 24-inch barrel and ventilated rib to enable me to draw quickly on fast-moving grouse. It would be choked improved cylinder and modified because the wide spray from an improved cylinder is especially forgiving to marginal wingshots like me. It would, of course, be a double-barreled boxlock since there is less chance for malfunction with the less sophisticated design than the design of a sidelock, pump, or repeater.

A 20-gauge of ultralight design would be my ultimate choice—by virtue of its featherweight and maneuverability—for a most effective grouse gun. I would also prefer a straight grip—as opposed to a pistol grip—which allows the shooter to mount the gun faster and gives quick access to double triggers. The straight grip doesn't fit the construction of the hand as well as its pistol grip counterpart when a hunter is merely carrying the gun through cover, but when you raise the gun to cheek, the grip fits your hand perfectly.

With the advent of adjustable choke systems to help govern the shot distribution or spread, short-barreled guns aren't necessarily open-choked, but a short barrel is, in my covert-tested opinion, a necessity. What is my definition of a short barrel, you ask? Anything less than 26 inches. The best grouse coverts are often those that can scarcely be traversed. There is perhaps nothing more hilarious in the world of sport than the sight of a gun-laden grouse hunter trying to hurry to a dog on point in a typical alder-choked thicket. Before the branches release the hunter from their grip, the thunderous flush of a grouse can be heard just beyond the pointer, somewhere out of sight. Negotiating such coverts with a long-barreled shotgun is much like duck hunting in a bass boat.

With that said, let me confess that my first experience grouse hunting came as a kid during a trip to southwestern Wisconsin. My armament was a full-choked, 30-inch-barreled Remington Model 870. To this day, I wonder how many of these guns were turned into anchor weights or fence posts by their owners. Functionally, the 870 is one of the finest pump shotguns on the market. The combination of a 30-inch barrel and full-choke (intended for *long*-distance shooting), however, was the inverse of good grouse gun characteristics. Now it's hardly fair to blame such a gun for poor results in grouse shooting, since its function was to fit the needs of waterfowlers, not upland bird hunters. However, even when I used the gun for waterfowl hunting, I found it cumbersome and simply couldn't think of a truly good use for such a gun, save as a cane should one twist a knee while picking up decoys. The point is, of course, that the time for such guns has gone the way of the wooden decoy.

Some hunters complain that they have difficulty swinging short-barreled guns smoothly. To that I reply that they are wise to forget about swinging on grouse—I cannot recall the last grouse that showed itself long enough for me to actually make a calculating swing. Grouse hunting gave rise to the term "snap shooting." This is a game in which the best hunters instantaneously locate potential shooting avenues at the first sound of a flushing grouse. A shooting avenue does not necessarily constitute a clearing. It is most likely a place where only a few leaves shield an escaping grouse from view—this is particularly true during the early season when foliage is dense. The hunter who waits for a clear shot at a grouse ought to try duck hunting.

Moreover, a hunter who doesn't carry a gun at port arms while in a birdy-looking covert is either an exceptional wingshot, does not recognize prime habitat, or has never tried to hit a ruffed grouse. I would bet a good bird dog that the person is a combination of the latter two. It is this kind of hunter who is responsible for educating grouse. The rest of us, of course, are then given the challenge of trying to stalk a bird that has heard the sound of BBs whizzing past its hide. Plenty of grouse become gun-shy from alert hunters; there's no need for haphazard nimrods to further the birds' education.

## FROM THE GUN RACK

Grouse hunters spend nearly as much time talking about their shotguns as they do their dogs. There are momentous and memorable guns passed from one generation to the next. There are also new guns with special appeal, worth saving to acquire. To some, these guns become far more than mere tools with which to kill grouse; indeed, they are part of the overall aesthetic appeal of grouse hunting. The beauty of some guns is merely in their simplicity of function; of others, in their fine checkering or custom engraving. Whatever your fancy, here's a look at a selection of guns that have, for one reason or another, found their way into many grouse hunters' homes.

**Beretta Onyx Series:** The corrosion-resistant matte finish separates these doubles from the rest of the Beretta shotguns. This is a working line of over-and-unders as well as side-by-sides that are also pleasant to the eye. Receivers on all the guns in the series are fully enclosed to keep dirt and residue from penetrating the action. They are also equipped with what Beretta calls its "Mobilchoke" screw-in choke system.

This Italian firm was founded by Bartolomeo Beretta shortly after 1500, thus making it the world's oldest industrial enterprise. The company operates a manufacturing facility in Accokeek, Maryland, but that plant chiefly produces handguns—all shotgun production remains in Brescia, Italy.

**Browning BPS and Citori:** I have a special bias to which I must admit before I delve any further into shotgun selections. Being a left-hand shooter, I tend to favor gun models that come in either left- or right-hand versions. Manufacturers who fail to offer guns designed for south-paw shooters are sending a message to me and other lefties—whether they realize it or not—that they don't care if they get our business. That is one reason I favor double guns.

Browning BPS, however, is what I might call an ambidextrous pump. The gun ejects its shells from the bottom, making it equally suitable for either right- or left-handed shooters. The BPS Upland Special is at home in any grouse thicket. The gun shares similarities with Remington's Special Field 870: It also has a 22-inch barrel and straight grip stock. It's light, quick, and easy to mount, but, like the 870 Special Field, its short barrel makes it loud. Because of this, light field loads are all I would shoot from either of these guns, so beware of mixing leftover pheasant shells with your grouse battery. The invector screw-in choke system comes standard with every BPS.

Browning Citori over-and-unders come in a variety of grades, but their Grade I Upland Special is the sweetest grouse gun of the lot. A straight grip stock and 24-inch barrels are two features that make it such. The company has come a long way from John Browning's beginnings with the A-5 autoloader, and the Citori line is living proof.

**Ithaca Model 87:** This model is really a continuation of the Model 37—the first shotgun manufactured by Ithaca in 1937. The Model 87 is the only bottom-ejecting pump shotgun currently made in America. Its Ultralight version has a 25-inch barrel and, in 20 gauge, weighs a mere 5 pounds. Ithaca barrels are hammered from 11-inch round billets of steel—the way most good rifle barrels are made, but few, if any, shotguns. Indeed, the Ithaca is too often overlooked by the grouse hunter.

**Remington 870 Special Field:** The 870 today is *the* American pump gun—with all due respect to Winchester's venerable Model 12. Steve Bodio in his book, *Good Guns*, said of the Model 12, "It is conceivably the only graceful repeater ever made, with sweeping curves and machined connections that are, sadly, too expensive to make anymore."

But Browning, of all companies, revived the Model 12 for a brief manufacturing engagement in which 12,000 guns were produced. Though it will never replace the sentimental old Model 12, the new counterpart is faithful to specifications and configurations of stock style, checkering, and detailing that were offered throughout the old 12's history.

The 870, nevertheless, has many virtues, too. Most notably, it is a functionally sound pump that will fit most any budget—the two greatest reasons for its popularity. The Special Field version of the model offers all the features a grouse hunter would want in a gun: short barrel, straight grip, center bead, and lightweight construction. There is nothing extravagant about these guns, but they have won a loyal following among pump fans. If you must have an autoloader, however, Remington offers its popular 1100 series in Special Field configuration as well.

**Ruger Red Label:** Although there are scores of fine European doubles, as of this printing there remains only one American-made over-and-under. But Ruger's Red Label is truly a damn fine over-and-under and, at $800, is affordable, too. The gun's receiver, trigger, and fore-end iron are made of stainless steel with a brushed-satin finish coming standard. The trigger guard, top lever, and safety thumbpiece, as well as barrels, are made of heat-treated chrome-molybdenum steels. It can also be had with 26-inch barrels and an assortment of screw-in chokes—making it perfectly adequate for most grouse hunters.

**The Old and New SKB:** Perhaps the friendliest gun I own is a honey of a 20-gauge SKB. This gun invites a hunter to carry it, point it, and ultimately shoot it. It's a leftover from Ithaca's affiliation with SKB of Tokyo and Tomobe, Japan. The venture began in 1966 and was enormously successful. Ithaca provided dandy doubles for stateside wingshots who showed their approval at the gun-counter cash register.

A falling-out between Ithaca and SKB, however, brought an end to the gun's import until Ernie Simmons (as in Simmons Optics) reintroduced them. The most noticeable difference between old and new is the improved wood and finish found in the new SKBs. The new side-by-sides are smooth-swinging, handsome productions, but it's still possible to fetch one of the old Ithaca SKBs by checking gun shows and gun tabloids. Moreover, most of the old SKBs can be found in the $500 to $800 range—perhaps the best buy in doubles around.

**Weatherby Orion:** While Weatherby's forte remains rifles, its venture into the shotgun market shouldn't go unnoticed by the grouse hunter. Weatherby's Orion model would fall into the category of versatile over-and-under, and there's nothing wrong with that. Its shortest barrel length is 26 inches, but it weighs a comfortable 6½ pounds. Part of the Orion's versatility lies in its screw-in chokes. Overall, the sturdy boxlock design makes the Orion an effective choice for most upland birds, including grouse.

# The Right Gun and Load

*If kids, mortgage payments or any other monetary drains affect your budget so that you have to carefully plan the purchase of a shotgun, the practical thing to do is to settle for one gun and learn to shoot it well.*

—David Michael Duffey, *Bird Hunting Tactics*

# The Right Gun and Load

Selecting the best load for a particular grouse or woodcock hunt is to upland gunning what matching the hatch is to fly-fishing. The degree to which you pay attention to details is very likely the extent to which you will enjoy success. This is painfully apparent to me when I venture into grouse coverts without having stopped to consider special conditions that may affect my shooting. Instead, I ceremoniously heap everything I think I need to take on the outing in the middle of the living room floor. To the pile, alas, I add the Remington Special Field 870 shotgun and two boxes of leftover shells loaded with No. 8 shot.

Then, of course, I venture into a fog-draped aspen thicket where a slight mist is falling. The grouse are perched like crows in the treetops instead of on the ground because any movement at that lower level would shake even more water on them from moisture-laden ferns and briars. The soft underfeathers of a grouse do a better job of absorbing water than repelling it. Everything in the woods is a dull collage of grays, blacks, and browns. Without a hint of a grouse's presence from my setter, a ruff launches from above, shaking a shower of water on my noggin as if to scorn my presence. The bird has a considerable head start, and my only shot comes as the bird eclipses an opening forty yards away. No feathers.

That was only the first bird of a whole string of treetop flushes that accounted for a most frustrating outing. The Remington 870 I happened to be using was bored improved cylinder and was manufactured before Remington made the guns standard with the adjustable Rem-choke. My loads were filled with an ounce of No. 8 shot with a measly 3¼ drams of powder propelling them. It was, to be sure, an entirely inadequate combination for fast-flying, distant grouse. Although I may not have experienced different results had I been using a gun with a changeable choke system, I would have at least felt better dressed for the occasion. Bird hunters have found adjustable chokes an important development—somewhere on the order of the advent of gunpowder.

A modified choke along with 1¼ ounces of No. 7½ shot and 3¾ drams of powder would have equaled roasted grouse—at least I humor myself by thinking such. This combination would have increased my effective killing range. Sporting the right gun and load recipe only slightly raises a hunter's chances of hitting a grouse that's using a tree branch as a springboard. Aficionados of sporting clays know the challenge of treetop flushing grouse from their reports at the shooting station called the duck tower. It is perhaps the most difficult shot in all of shotgundom. What makes such a shot so difficult is that grouse, unlike clay targets, dive from a tree branch using their free-fall to accelerate—in essence, they are using gravity instead of fighting it. Not only is the grouse losing altitude, it is also gaining velocity. The amount of guesswork involved in judging the rate at which the bird is both falling and accelerating is often monumental—as in insurmountable. Since clay birds lose speed from the moment they are flung, simple physics dictates that they will never perfectly simulate the burst of flight speed associated with many upland game birds.

## WOODCOCK AT CLOSE RANGE

The shooting equation is further complicated when woodcock enter the picture. Suppose, for instance, that it is the early season and migrating timberdoodles have recently invaded your favorite grouse covert. After three consecutive grouse flushes, it is easy to be fooled by the slower flight change-up of a woodcock. Make no mistake, however; woodcock are anything but easy targets. Although biologists who study such things tell us that woodcock fly slower than grouse and grouse slower than pheasant, speed has very little to do with a woodcock's ability to evade birdshot. A hunter may hunt all three of these birds and, given the right conditions, have time to empty a three-shot pump before any of these three species are able to get out of range.

Woodcock, more than any other bird I have hunted on three continents, have an innate ability to change their flight speeds not once, not twice, but many times throughout the course of a single flush. Some woodcock burst out with all the fury their compact breast muscles can generate. Others simply flutter above the alders like overgrown moths where they hover for a moment before ever so dainti-

Having a dog locate a grouse is only part of the hunt. Shooting with tree limbs filling the firmament adds an aura of impossibility—making a clean kill all the more rewarding. (*Photo* © *by John Kubisiak*)

Although some ruffed grouse allow a dog to approach within a foot or two before flushing, others escape at the first hint of oncoming dogs or hunters. Such inconsistency accounts for much of the challenge in grouse hunting. (*Photo © by Tom Martinson*)

Some hardmouthed dogs are trained to point dead or wounded birds like this setter is doing in a Michigan covert. The well-camouflaged grouse is difficult to find on the forest floor, making good dogs invaluable in retrieving downed birds. (*Photo © by Chris Dorsey*)

The best grouse dogs are exposed to birds early and often. This setter pup owned by Gary Wilson became a productive hunter during his second season, and blossomed into a fine grouse dog during his third year. (*Photo © by Chris Dorsey*)

It's usually best to approach any pointing dog from the side. By so doing, you increase your chances of getting a shot at the bird, and such a practice allows the dog to maintain visual contact with you, thus calming it in an otherwise tense moment. (*Photo © by Bob Robb*)

Phil Brodbeck and the author combined for four grouse, two woodcock, and a ringneck rooster in an afternoon hunt in Wisconsin. It takes an experienced dog to find and point all three species in a single outing. (*Photo © by Chris Dorsey*)

German shorthairs are the most popular of the continental breeds used for grouse hunt-ing. What they lack in style and flash they make up for in bird-finding instincts. (*Photo © by Bob Robb*)

Beeper collars such as this one manufactured by Tri-Tronics are a handy improvement over the conventional dog bell. The collar changes its cadence when the dog stops on point, thus signaling the hunter where the dog and bird are located. (*Photo © by Chris Dorsey*)

The English setter is the classic choice for grouse hunting. Its long hair is an asset, protecting it from the thorns and brambles so common throughout most good grouse habitat. (*Photo © by Bob Robb*)

This Orvis lanyard combines a dog whistle, compass, and counters that allow hunters to tally the number of grouse and woodcock flushes made in a single outing. (*Photo © by Dave Hetzler*)

Thick grouse cover is no place for dogs who won't retrieve. The edge of an alder thicket and cornfield provided Phil Brodbeck an opportunity at a midwestern ruff. (*Photo © by Chris Dorsey*)

Ardent Georgia grouse hunter Aaron Pass is one of a small number of Peach State grouse hunters. Hunters in this part of the grouse's range rely on dogs like the author's setter to find what few birds inhabit the region. (*Photo © by Chris Dorsey*)

The best grouse pointers are able to locate bird scent from a great distance and establish a point without spooking skittish grouse. This stylish setter shows it is one such dog during a Pennsylvania field trial. (*Photo © by Dave Fletcher*)

Well-trained grouse dogs, like these two grouse trial winners, are a valuable commodity in the uplands. There is perhaps no greater challenge for a pointing dog than a ruffed grouse. (*Photo © by Dave Fletcher*)

ly landing twenty feet from where the dog just spooked them. There's nothing so frustrating as a bird that won't play by the rules.

"Flush like a real bird, you hideous imp!" I scold as I empty both barrels of my SKB without the bird so much as even noticing—as if tree branches routinely explode in its face. Hell hath no fury like a bird hunter scorned. To further irritate me, the bird continued these short leaps until I had laid to waste scores of young aspen and a half a box of shells. With each miss at what appeared an easy target, my resolve to kill this beast grew until, alas, he fluttered to the grand peenting ground in the sky.

"Take that!"

The woodcock undoubtedly would have succumbed far sooner had I, first, not lost my patience and, second, been using the right gun and load combination. Some of my shots came at ten paces. I hate to think what would have become of the bird had I connected at that close range with the modified barrel. In this case, double-barrel skeet choke with one ounce of No. 8 shot or even No. 9 would have been superior to my improved modified and No. 7½ shot.

The Orvis company, the Manchester, Vermont-based manufacturer of equipment for upland bird hunting, has only recently developed a unique shotshell for woodcock hunting. The Spreader Loads, as they are called, use flat, disc-shaped shot instead of conventional round pellets. How do these loads perform differently than standard field shells, you ask? They establish a remarkably wide pattern at short range. The flat shot tumbles and spins through the air in anything but a uniform manner, which is why it develops a wide pattern at short range. These loads have a lengthy shot string—the distance between the first pellet to arrive on target and the last—which makes them all the more forgiving for the marginal shot. While they aren't recommended for shooting much beyond twenty yards, I can think of no better load for woodcock hunting in heavy cover—the only cover in which woodcock are ever found. They are particularly effective in double-barrel shotguns because a hunter can use the Spreader Loads in the open barrel and use conventional No. 7½ or No. 8 shot in the modified barrel, thereby maximizing the chance of hitting at almost any range.

## LONG-DISTANCE GROUSE

For an entirely different scenario, suppose for a moment that it is two days before Christmas and you've promised in-laws that you would provide four grouse for Christmas dinner. You guaranteed them you would supply the birds after your pugnacious brother-in-law challenged in front of everyone that you and your fumbling pointer couldn't deliver the birds unless the local flock of ruffs were suddenly stricken with polio.

Confident that four birds will be no problem, you feast on the birds taken earlier in the season and decide to wait until the last week before Christmas to begin hunting for the holiday meal. You can taste the sweetness of revenge. But after two days of traipsing the snow-covered hills, you have only the glimpse of three wild-flushing birds to show for it. Several hours of telephone calls to local game farms reveal that no one raises the birds and that your only recourse is to sheepishly offer a turkey in lieu of the promised grouse. That idea evaporates, however, the moment the thought of your grinning brother-in-law cooks in your mind.

Instead, you concentrate on potting those four birds yourself. Since every one you've spotted in the last two days has flushed at the fringe of shotgun range, your only chance is to replace your improved and modified chokes with modified and full bore to increase the gun's long-distance killing effectiveness. Most of the vegetation is off the leaves now, allowing you ample visibility at distant ranges. You solicit a sympathetic friend for your cause and promise him the pick of the litter from your champion bitch's next litter.

You know where there's a small grove of spruce that has traditionally held grouse during the late season, but it is an hour's hike just to reach it and it is a gamble whether or not the birds will be there. If the birds are there, however, they will be in flocks. You position yourself on a slope overlooking the young spruce where you guess that your modified-full choked double and No. 6 shot will be the perfect choice for taking distant birds. Now you signal your buddy to start walking the thicket toward you, with dog vacuuming the leaves in front of him. Shortly after he begins the drive, grouse flush from the trees, towering past you....

Two days later, everyone except your brother-in-law is eating grouse; instead, he consumes a plate of crow—served cold, of course.

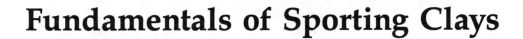

# Fundamentals of Sporting Clays

*I'll lay my money on bringing home a passing bluebill or rising woodcock before I'd wager on bagging a flushed grouse.*
—Tom Anderson, "Drumming An Old Tune"

# Fundamentals of Sporting Clays

A decade ago, the game of sporting clays—also known as hunter's clays—was as foreign to American shotgunners as driven partridge shoots. Today, however, this British invasion is well entrenched as over two hundred sporting clays courses have been built across America. This game, more than any other clay sport devised to date, closely approximates the actual shooting conditions a hunter might encounter afield.

At last!—a shooting game especially for hunters! It is because of this game that many hunters no longer shun the arena of clay target shooting. Each clays layout, like a golf course, is unique in its design. There are, in fact, many similarities in the way in which the two kinds of courses are constructed. Both should be designed to be challenging, but not so difficult that they dishearten beginning shooters. In either case, it takes an experienced hand to go about developing both an interesting and challenging course.

The sport of clays was invented in merry old England where gentry humored away their days by shooting live birds until their barrels warped, along with their sense of humor. When the time came that birds grew scarce and peasants founded unions, clay targets were substituted for live birds. Incidentally, the first clay target was the product of Yankee ingenuity. George Ligowski devised the clay pigeon, as the story goes, after watching children skip clam shells across a lake. Today, the game is Britain's second most popular participatory sport, ranking a close second behind angling.

As presently the fastest-growing shooting sport in the United States, clays may one day surpass both trap and skeet in order of popularity, though that day is still in the distant future. Aside from its obvious appeal to hunters seeking a game that simulates wingshooting, sporting clays is attractive to many because it is relatively inexpensive to develop an informal clays course—especially when compared to the cost of conventional trap and skeet ranges.

Sporting courses vary greatly in size and scope. Some offer numerous different stations, while others of the backyard variety may only have a few—birds are then shot from different angles to maximize the amount of shooting practice offered at each. Sporting clays has already garnered an avid following of shooters who do little but shoot clay games. The problem with this as I see it is that—as in trap and skeet—the original intent of the game is skewed because winning the game takes priority over improving wingshooting. Indeed, shooters buy specially made guns and change choke tubes at each station in an attempt to win competitive shoots, not to improve their field shooting. The result, some fear, is that the game will evolve into a highly competitive sport like trap and skeet and will no longer be a practice game for hunters who simply want to improve their wingshooting.

A hunter interested in improving his or her wingshooting skills has only to keep this purpose in mind when shooting clays. Some sporting shoots are dubbed "fun" shoots in an attempt to ease the pressure of competition that naturally seems to surface in almost any American activity. If your purpose is to be able to hit grouse on a semiconsistent basis, then use your grouse gun during the shoot and forget about changing choke tubes between stations. If you're attempting to simulate field shooting, consider any number of factors and equipment you use to complete a successful wingshot. If, for instance, you often wear shooting gloves and glasses while hunting, you should wear them during sporting shoots as well. Try to recreate hunting conditions as closely as possible.

In trap and skeet, the shooter always knows—to one degree or another—exactly where the target will be thrown. By simple repetition, a shooter can learn to break targets consistently. Since sporting clays courses are unique, shooters are never given the chance to groove a particular shot. Birds may be flung from an infinite variety of placements—in fact, the more diverse the better. Singles, doubles, pairs of doubles, and sequential pairs can be thrown in any combination to fool even the best shooters. While perfect scores in trap and skeet can be as common as the cold, as of this writing only one man has ever shot a perfect game of competition sporting clays.

One of the rules of this game is that the shooter must start with the gun down, or with the gun stock positioned below the shooter's armpit. The gun cannot be brought to shoulder until the target is in sight of the shooter. The ideal sporting shooter uses the instinctive method whereby the eyes follow the target until the gun is mounted and fired in the *same* instant. This method is particularly British and is superior to raising the gun and then tracking the bird, as is common with American wingshots. Adding to the difficulty of the game is the fact that the bird may be thrown up to three seconds after the shooter calls for it. If that weren't enough, clay targets used in sporting clays come in six sizes. The minis, the smallest, are 60 millimeters across and look like silver dollars arcing through the air. Next in line is the midi target, a black disc measuring 90 millimeters across. The midi is followed by the rabbit, a 100-millimeter clay that's bounced on its edge along the ground. A battue target is 110 milimeters and is pancake flat. The standard and rocket targets are roughly the same size as the battue.

In organized sporting clays events, shooters are grouped in teams of roughly five. The teams rotate to different stations which offer a variety of shooting angles. A round of competition normally consists of one hundred targets, but recreational shoots offer any number of different shot and station combinations. Twelve-gauge over-and-under shotguns are used most often during tournaments, but again, the hunter interested in improving wingshooting ability ought to use the same gun taken afield.

Anything larger than the .410 bore can be used to shoot the various stations in a sporting course—though I've seen a handful of skilled shooters successfully use a .410. Each station is given the name of a species of bird which indicates the type of shot that the station tries to provide. Clay targets flung straight into the air, for instance, are called "springing teal." One of the beauties of clays, remember, is that each course is unique, so there will undoubtedly be many local and regional differences in the names of similar stations. A "dove tower" in the South may be called a "duck tower" in the Midwest, for example. But here are a few of the more common shots shooters are likely to encounter on a quintessential sporting clays course.

**Driven Pheasants:** This is usually an overhead shot for which the birds are thrown from a tower or hillside directly above the shooters. Depending on the height of the tower or hill, the birds can be moderate to very high. Most successful shooters swing on these targets until the barrel has moved past the clay and the target is blocked from sight by the passing barrels. The instant the barrels eclipse the target, squeeze the trigger.

**Springing Teal:** This is a clay subspecies of the migratory fowl known only to the sporting shooter. Two birds are thrown simultaneously straight into the air in an attempt to simulate two teal rising off a pond. Some shooters advocate taking the birds on the rise, while other prefer to wait until the targets slow at the peak of their rise.

**Fur and Feather:** This is usually a combination of crossing targets. One is a specially hardened target that is rolled or bounced on its edge along the ground to simulate running game. The bounces of these clay bunnies are as unpredictable as the leaps of the wild variety. The second shot typically involves a low crossing bird flung from the opposite direction of the rabbit so that the shooter must swing both to the left and to the right.

**Streaking Chukars (or what I might call Tree-Launched Grouse):** Here the targets are thrown either from left to right or from right to left through cover. If the station is designed correctly, the challenge will be to locate an optimum shooting lane before the birds are out of range.

**Decoying Duck:** A pair of battue targets are thrown over a pond (or on land on some courses) and curl toward the water as they fall at the end of their flight. Since the battue target is flat, it is difficult to break on edge, so most shooters wait until the birds begin to drop to the water before shooting, when the target has exposed more surface area to the shooter.

# Grouse Shooting or
# Tree Pruning?

*A partridge goes off from amid the pitch pines. It lifts each wing so high above its back and flaps so low, and withal so rapidly, that they present the appearance of a broad wheel, almost a revolving sphere, as it whirs off like a cannon-ball shot from a gun.*

—Henry David Thoreau

# Grouse Shooting or Tree Pruning?

**A** walk through an alder jungle can intimidate wingshots— particularly those whose only shotgunning experience has taken place in the wide-open expanse of a duck slough or dove field. After a budding hunter hears six consecutive grouse flushes without so much as catching a single glimpse of a bird, the task of bringing a ruff to hand can seem more a matter of holy intervention than shotgunning prowess.

Contrary to popular belief, however, grouse are not extraordinarily strong flying birds. Their wings are short and compact, a design best suited to negotiate the herbaceous environs they inhabit. Their wings give them a short, explosive burst of speed, but they cannot maintain that speed like a dove or duck. On the other hand, they seldom have to, as within a few wingbeats a grouse will have quickly put cover between itself and the shooter. Long, calculating swings of the gun and body toward the bird—the fancy of pass-shooters—are best left in a duck or dove blind. A hunter must first understand that the longer a grouse is in flight, the greater are its chances of flying behind cover and out of sight. The goal of a grouse shooter, generally, is to shoot the bird as quickly as possible. A hunter who hesitates wastes shells. A hunter who waits for a ruff to fly through a clearing and offer a shot is one who has spent little time in grouse cover.

## INSTINCTIVE SHOOTING

Lest you think successful grouse shooting requires a mix of Zen and mental telepathy, there is a method of instinctive shooting that will bolster your chances of hitting grouse, or any other bird you happen to be stalking. This instinctive method— sometimes called the Churchill method after its developer, Robert Churchill (also the author of the classic *Game Shooting*)—is a product of British shooting. Despite the ingenuity of Yanks, it is a method that has yet to be improved upon by American wingshots.

American shotgunners most commonly mount the gun, look to the bead of the gun, and swing through the target before shooting. British wingshots locate the target first, following it closely with their eyes. They then mount the gun and shoot in the same instant, paying little attention to the location of the bead. If the gun is cheeked properly according to this method, your body swing and line of sight will automatically—or instinctively—bring the gun barrel in position to kill the bird. In fact, a bead on a shotgun becomes virtually obsolete when shooting instinctively since your eye focuses on the target, not the gun.

Bruce Bowlen, former director of the Orvis Shooting Schools where he taught wingshooting methods for twelve years, writes in his *Orvis Wing-Shooting Handbook* that the "single most important rule in field shooting is to keep your eye on the bird and not the barrel." His advice underlies the fundamental difference between the way most Americans are taught shotgunning and the way in which Brits approach the same sport.

Now consider trap and skeet shooters who shoulder their shotguns before the target is even thrown. By so doing, they are training themselves to focus down the barrel of the gun instead of at the target at which they are about to shoot. When your target travels a predictable flight path at a given speed, it typically makes very little difference in the end result since most shooters are able to shoot at a predetermined location in the target's flight path.

The problem comes when trap and skeet shooters apply the techniques they have learned at the range to wingshooting. By having to mount the gun and center the bead before shooting, they are wasting valuable time—a most precious commodity when in a grouse thicket. Ironically, trap and skeet shooters premount their shotguns as a way to expedite the shooting process, but ultimately in the field they are losing time by first locating the bead of their shotguns, then the birds they are trying to shoot. With practice, the instinctive method becomes something of a natural shooting reflex—simple enough not to encumber the shooter during the instant of a grouse flush.

The reason this method works so well for grouse hunters is that it teaches shooters to adapt to any shooting situation they may face. Grouse hunting, perhaps more than any other form of bird hunting, offers a hunter the widest array of shooting angles. Think for a moment. What are the shots that give you the most difficulty? If a high crossing shot was the only opportunity I'd ever had on grouse, I could say with some confidence that I would have yet to kill a bird. That shot, thankfully, represents a small percentage of my shots on grouse. Other wretched souls have the misfortune of not being able to hit grouse moving straight away.

The instinctive method, however, offers maligned wingshots a chance at redemption if they confess their shooting sins. For trap and skeet aficionados who have had difficulty making a transition to live targets—those that don't flush from the same source or fly in a predictable speed and direction—the instinctive method offers wingshooting salvation. After years of clay bird shooting, ardent trap and skeet shooters, however, often have difficulty making adjustments to the instinctive method. Though the conversion is often difficult, it is by no means impossible. The born-again wingshot need not be an especially talented sort, only a persistent one.

The instinctive method is truly so simple that it can hardly be called a method at all. In fact, the use of "method" implies that it requires cognitive effort to use this shooting technique. For the grouse hunter, first examine your approach to game. How do you carry your gun? This fundamental question goes unanswered by most wingshots. It is important not to walk with the barrel raised above your line of sight. According to Churchill, a gun should be carried with the buttstock between the upper arm and chest, the left hand on the fore-end or barrels (if shooting right-handed), and the muzzle(s) pointing slightly skyward straight in front of the shooter. An object even the size of a gun barrel can block a significant portion of your field of view. The goal of proper gun carry is to allow the shooter to mount the gun with a minimum of motion. There is no time to waste when trying to intercept grouse, so efficiency of motion is critical to quick shooting.

## GUN FIT

The use of the English instinctive method is predicated on having a gun that fits the shooter properly. Since an instinctive shooter isn't cognizant of a gun's bead during the shooting process, the eye must align perfectly over the gun barrel in order to hit game. The stock, therefore, must fit a shooter in such a way as to automatically bring the eye and gun barrel in line.

While most shooters can achieve a certain degree of proficiency with run-of-the-mill factory shotguns, shooting with a well-fitted gun—like using the correct tool—increases the chances of doing your job correctly. To fit a gun, a gun maker must know the appropriate shooting dimensions of the shooter. A device called a try gun is used to derive these measurements. The try gun has adjustable parts that are moved until the shooter feels comfortable with the fit and the eye is aligned with the gun barrel. In other words, adjustments are made on the gun until the gun shoots where the shooter is pointing. From this point, measurements are taken from different parts of the try gun, and a custom gun fit is then determined. With these measurements, a gun maker carves a stock to specially conform to your body build.

Drop at comb, drop at heel, length of pull, and pitch aren't dance steps; they're four important gun measurements needed to custom-fit your gun. Many sporting-goods dealers will look quizzically at you if you request to be measured for gun fit, but specialty gun shops and Orvis outlets will likely be able to help you.

## DOMINANT EYE

I once entered into a debate with a gun manufacturer over the percentage of left-hand versus right-hand shooters in America. While the gun representative recited his statistics that only a small percentage of Americans are left-handed, I couldn't help but wonder about those shooters—like me—who are right-handed, but left-eye dominant. Eye dominance, of course, refers to a person's eye that is most accurate when picturing an image. It behooves a shooter to use the best eye when focusing on a flying bird. Of six shooters on staff at *Hunting* magazine where I work, one is left-handed, left-eye dominant, and shoots left-handed. I am right-handed but shoot left-handed because I am left-eye dominant. Two others are right-handed but left-eye dominant, and they shoot right-handed, while two are right-handed, right-eye dominant, and shoot right-handed. This is to say that four of the six shooters are left-eye dominant and, therefore, should shoot left-handed for best results. While this is by no means representative of the rest of the shooting world, it illustrates the many variables common to shotgunning. Over the years I have made an informal survey of shooters and am quite confident the number of left-eye dominant shooters is, in all likelihood, far greater than the 15 to 25 percent of Americans who are reportedly left-handed.

The significance of this is that left-eye-dominant shooters for years have been mistakenly taught to shoot right-handed. These shooters, thus, are condemned to never fully realize their shooting potential. This isn't to say that left-eye-dominant shooters cannot learn to shoot right-handed, but by the same token a person who walks with a limp will never win the Boston Marathon.

Moreover, my conversations with representatives from the gun industry lead me to believe that they have surprisingly little data about the number of left-eye-dominant shooters. That's a curious fact when one considers that the very livelihood of gun manufacturers depends on such information. The result for left-handed shooters is that—with few exceptions—gun makers have skewed their productions disproportionately to favor right-handed shooters.

Historically, hunters learned to shoot shotguns left- or right-handed based solely on whether or not they were left- or right-handed. Now, however, most hunter safety curriculums test beginning shooters for left- or right-eye dominance, thereby teaching them at an early age to correctly shoot left- or right-handed based on eye dominance. Since these courses are now mandatory in most states, there has been a growing percentage of left-handed shooters in America, and the number will increase as long as hunters are taught early to shoot the way their bodies are designed, not the way guns are built.

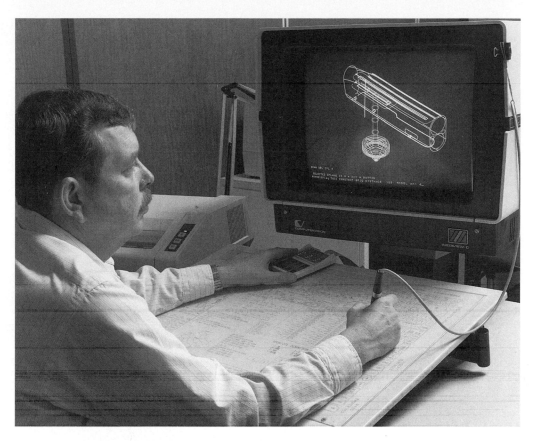

Tom Plunkett, research designer, uses Remington's computer-aided design system to detail a receiver for a new generation of Remington shotguns. (*Photo courtesy Dick Dietz, Remington Arms*)

Beretta Onyx Series

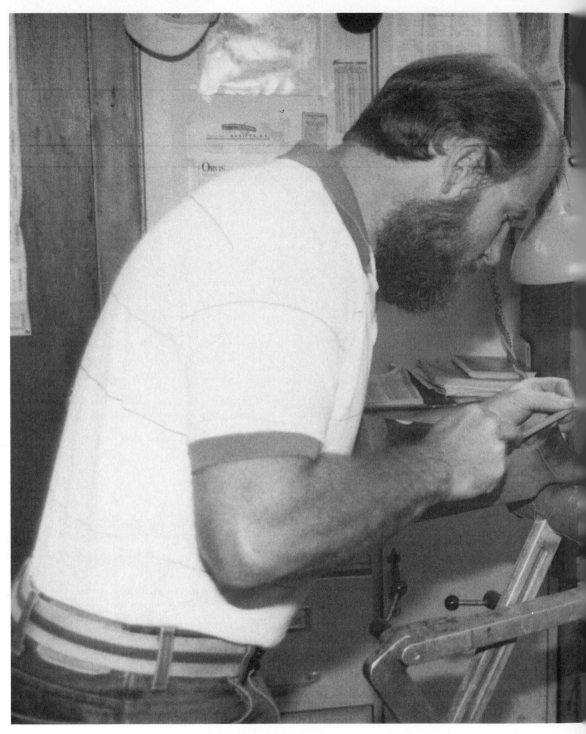

A gunsmith can often make slight alterations in your shotgun's stock that will improve its fit to your cheek and shoulder. (*Photo © by Chris Dorsey*)

The Remington Model 870 pump is America's best-selling shotgun. In the Special Field configuration, the gun provides grouse hunters with an effective pump. (*Photo © by Chris Dorsey*)

Boxlock, sidelock, over-and-under, side-by-side, pump, auto—shoot as many as possible before settling with one gun. Short–barreled, open-choked guns are the rage of most grouse hunters. (*Photo © by Chris Dorsey*)

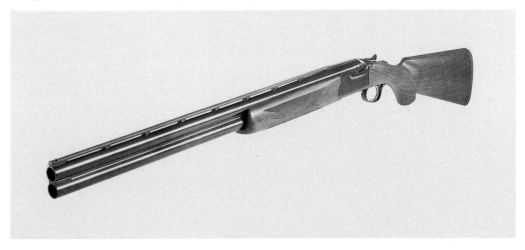

Ruger Red Label.

Ruger Red Label.

George Bird Evans's Belton setters are nearly as famous as his Purdy. (*Photo* © *by David L. Hall*)

Remington Model 1100 LT-20 "Special."

Browning's reintroduction of the Model 12 pump in 28 gauge.

Browning Citori 12 gauge.

Selecting the grade of wood to be used on a custom double is an event to be savored. (*Photo © by Chris Dorsey*)

Late in the season when the majority of leaves have fallen from the trees and shots at grouse become increasingly distant, many hunters change from No. 8 or 9 shot to the larger No. 7½'s. (*Photo © byChris Dorsey*)

The dense foliage typical of early-season grousing makes open-choked guns preferable for generally close-range shooting. (*Photo © by Chris Dorsey*)

Short-barreled guns have won a large following among grouse and woodcock hunters because of their improved maneuverability in heavy cover. (*Photo © by Bob Robb*)

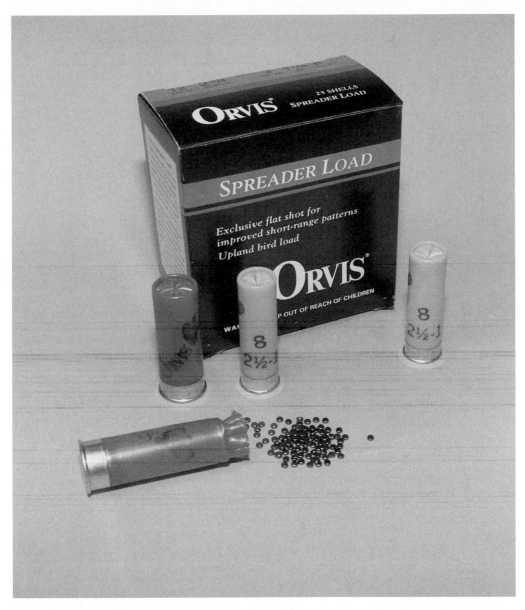

A unique idea in shotgunning is Orvis's use of flat shot in a load designed for close-range grouse and woodcock shooting. (*Photo © by Dave Hetzler*)

While British shotgunners have long enjoyed the game of sporting clays, it has only recently gained widespread popularity in America. One of its many attractions is its close approximation to actual wingshooting—an area in which both trap and skeet fall short. (*Photo © by Chris Dorsey*)

This "Driven Grouse" blind is just one of an unlimited number of different stations wingshots might encounter on a sporting clays course. Each clay's range—like a golf course—is unique, adding to the game's appeal. (*Photo © by Chris Dorsey*)

# Two Perils in the Coverts

*In the north country, the ruffed grouse and its odd-looking little sidekick, the woodcock, remain about the last challenge for the hunter who would rather gun a true sporting bird than eat, sleep or make love.*

—David Michael Duffey, *Bird Hunting Tactics*

# Two Perils in the Coverts

## LYME DISEASE

Ticks, ticks, those bedeviling ticks! These tiny parasites have captured national attention in recent years as they spread Lyme Disease across the land in a modern-day plague. Several species of small ticks, including the well-known deer tick, transmit Lyme Disease. While the adult forms are about 3 millimeters, or half the size of a wood tick, and carry Lyme Disease, it is the tiny nymph forms, the size of a pinhead, that are largely responsible for transmitting the spirochetes causing the disease. "The disease of the 1990s," some say. One health bulletin I read recently claimed that "if it weren't for AIDS, Lyme Disease would have been the most talked about illness of the 1980s."

As it turned out, however, Americans were showered with scores of news broadcasts and magazine articles about the ailment, anyway. All three major television networks devoted news time to the epidemic, and *Newsweek* even ran a photo of a horrendously enlarged tick on its cover. A tick of the size depicted on that cover wouldn't bother siphoning blood; rather, it would eat you limb by limb. They're hideous beasts. Their grotesque ugliness makes it all the more enjoyable to kill them. With much delight, I squash one and roll it between my index finger and thumb—not the way I would a cigar, but with mashing conviction.

As if their mere creepiness weren't enough, ticks have to exacerbate their deplorable existence by spreading illness to hunter and beast. The two setters currently in my kennel both have remnants of the Lyme spirochete flowing in their blood. Grousing trips to the Great Lakes states are shared not only with birds, but with ticks. A band across Wisconsin and Minnesota is currently the hotbed for the disease, though it is prevalent throughout the Midwest and New England—

and is quickly expanding its range. Georgia, for instance, had a reported four cases of Lyme in 1987, but in the first eleven months of 1989 alone, the state department of health had already logged 688 cases of the disease. Over 13,000 cases of Lyme have been diagnosed across the United States since 1980—6,000 cases alone were reported in 1988, more than double the number identified in 1987. It's a cruel coincidence that the highest concentration for the disease, however, happens to coincide with America's best grouse-hunting regions.

The illness was not even officially diagnosed until 1975, despite the fact that a similar disease was reported by a grouse hunter in Taylor County, Wisconsin, in 1969—the same county in which my two setters contracted the disease. Lyme derives its name from Old Lyme, the small town in Connecticut where it was first detected. Most common symptoms include headache, chills, fever, fatigue, a spreading rash, nausea, and aching joints, but over eighty different symptoms have been linked with the disease. It's a peculiar infection in that even without treatment symptoms may disappear, only to recur intermittently for several months. It's also believed—though not yet confirmed—that the Lyme spirochetes may be able to remain dormant in the body even after treatment, only to reappear months or even years later.

Approximately 80 percent of the people infected with the ailment will develop a red rash within three to thirty-two days after being bitten by an infected tick. The rash is normally oval in shape and may resemble a red bull's-eye on the skin, but is not always restricted to the site of the bite.

The key to treating the disease is early diagnosis. There are three clinical stages to Lyme, and patients receiving treatment during the initial stage are at lowest risk of developing complications later in life. Antibiotics such as tetracycline, erythromycin, and penicillin are most often used to treat the ailment. Because of what isn't yet known about the disease, however, doctors warn that preventing Lyme is a far better idea than relying on treatment to cure the infection.

Several weeks or months after initial exposure to the bacterium or after the first symptoms appear, some people may develop complications involving the nervous or cardiovascular system. Specific disorders may include varying degrees of heart block; nervous system abnormalities such as meningitis, facial paralysis, encephalitis; or other conditions involving peripheral nerves.

It's during the final stage of the disease that arthritis becomes the most typically recognized long-term ailment. Even years after their first symptoms appear, some people may experience repeated attacks of arthritis. Research has shown that even if Lyme Disease was not diagnosed and treated promptly, people who eventually received appropriate antibiotic therapy had fewer relapses than those who never received treatment.

The fact that you are now aware of the disease is perhaps your greatest defense against it. If you know a tick has bitten you, be certain to look for the symptoms outlined above. Consult your doctor should you develop these symptoms associated with Lyme. A blood test will positively reveal whether or not you have been infected with the bacterium.

Virtually all of my grouse-hunting companions have treated at least one of their bird dogs for the disease. Two friends, in fact, have undergone treatment themselves. One was diagnosed early and was successfully treated, suffering no lasting ill effects. The other had the misfortune of contracting the disease during the first years it was recognized. It took several months to properly diagnose his condition, but treatment came too late to eliminate lifelong complications. He now regularly experiences pain in swollen knee joints—the same joints that used to propel him through an aspen thicket like a well-conditioned athlete.

**Gun Dog Care:** Symptoms in dogs include fever of 103 to 106 degrees, sudden lameness, severe pain, intermittent lameness for weeks or months, and illness within a few days or up to several months after initial exposure. Dogs are treated with the same battery of antibiotics used with humans. Dogs exposed to several ticks in a region known to have the disease should be tested by a veterinarian. But this is where you may find some discrepancies among vets. After having my dogs tested on different occasions in Georgia, California, and Wisconsin, I've encountered vets who knew little if anything about the disease. While it may be understandable to a certain degree that vets in Georgia and California—places where the disease is yet relatively uncommon—may know little about the ailment, I discovered one Wisconsin vet who knew far less than even I did about the disease. Such shortcomings prove to be disconcerting when you're placing your dog's future in the hands of such a physician. In the regions most affected by the disease, however, the vast majority of veterinarians have already treated several cases of the infection and are well aware of symptoms and standard treatment regimens.

A limited number of testing centers across the continent accept blood samples sent by veterinarians all over North America to be tested for Lyme. With thousands of blood tests weekly, there are plenty of possible sources for error. I took both my setters to the vet for routine blood tests for Lyme, and during handling, the two samples were switched. After the setter testing negative to the disease had begun to limp and was ill, I realized I had been given medication to treat the wrong dog. Another trip to the vet and a blood test confirmed my suspicions, but only after the disease was given a chance to fester in the veteran's blood.

**Prevention:** By routinely checking each day for ticks on yourself and your dog after hunting, you can remove them before they embed and have a chance to transmit Lyme Disease—at least most of them, but never all of them. Dr. Jim Gill, a microbiologist at the University of Minnesota Hospitals, emphasizes that ticks, especially in the nymph stage, can be impossibly small to find until they feed and swell in size—and then transmission of the disease may have taken place.

Repellents with a minimum of 30 percent DEET are very effective in repelling many kinds of ticks and may be applied directly to your clothes and hunting dog. Permanone, an insect repellent manufactured by the Coulston International Corporation, is arguably the most effective tick repellent on the market. Permanone was developed jointly in cooperation with the U.S. military, U.S. Department of Agriculture, and Tennessee Valley Authority. Of scores of tick and insect repellents tested by the group, Permanone was the only product that proved to be 100 percent effective when properly applied to clothing or a dog's coat. Repel, a repellent manufactured by Wisconsin Pharmacal Company, can be used in concert with Permanone. While Permanone should only be applied to clothing, Repel is applied directly to the skin. By using Permanone on clothes and Repel on your skin, you are effectively providing two layers of protection against ticks. Use the sprays on your dog before and after being in the field. Also, realize that the ticks transmitting Lyme Disease become adults in September, persist into November, and are active on sunny winter days even in January—as Gill, a grouse hunter as well as a microbiologist, has observed.

As of this writing, Lyme Disease experts predict that it will take a minimum of five years to develop any sort of vaccine for the disease. In all likelihood, however, it may take longer. With the acceleration of research on Lyme, doctors have begun examining a myriad of causes and effects of the disease that often alter commonly held beliefs about the ailment. It is for that reason that prevention is presently the best way to cope with this disease about which little is actually known.

A handy wallet-sized tick identification card has been developed by Wisconsin Pharmacal Company and can be ordered free by writing them at P.O. Box 198, Jackson, Wisconsin 53037.

## BLASTOMYCOSIS

While few hunters have even heard of this fungal disease, it is a potentially lethal infection that is prevalent in some of America's best grouse range. In a report in the *American Journal of Epidemiology*, cases of blastomycosis in Wisconsin were studied during a period from the late 1970s to the '80s by Bruce S. Klein and Jeffrey P. Davis.

According to Klein and Davis, the disease is caused by the fungus *Blastomyces dermatitidis*. Symptoms are wide ranging, from pulmonary disease to a rapidly degenerative and fatal illness involving several organ systems. The most common symptom, though, is chronic pneumonia. Diagnosis of the disease can be accomplished either through a blood sample in which telltale antibodies will be present or through a culture designed to detect the fungus itself. It's a relatively rare form of infection and certainly poses much less hazard to hunters than does the threat of an auto wreck each time you change lanes on the freeway. It is, however, additive risk we are talking about—the potential to be squashed on the highway remains a constant danger as long as we rely on automobiles for transportation, while blastomycosis is an additional hazard.

In a 1986 report in *The New England Journal of Medicine*, several cases of blastomycosis were studied in an outbreak in northern Wisconsin. It was noted that "available clinical and epidemiologic evidence suggests that humans and animals usually acquire blastomycosis by the airborne route from a source in nature." In the study, several Wisconsin school children contracted the infection when they visited an environmental camp in the northern part of the state. Researchers studied the surrounding environs but were unable to pinpoint any one specific environmental condition that would have caused the outbreak of the disease. According to the University of Wisconsin's Dr. Klein, roughly seventy-five cases of the disease are reported in the state each year. That represents, he says, an underestimate of the actual number of cases found in Wisconsin.

Blastomycosis is insidious by nature, and cases of the infection have increased in recent years. The majority of cases in America occur along the Mississippi River basin and throughout the Great Lakes region. The moist bottomlands associated with this area are believed to provide the fungus with optimal growing conditions.

The disease appears to be most common in men, but too little data exists to conclusively prove that hypothesis. One study cited by Klein and Davis suggests that "the organism resides in nature where the soil is enriched by avian manure. A few small areas of very high risk are interspersed among large areas of land where the risk of infection is minimal. Exposure of hunters during bird hunting season may explain the apparent increase in cases seen in winter months, and January may be the period of highest incidence for the diagnosis of the disease. The reason for this is because the reported incubation interval ranges from 33 to 44 days and, at least in Minnesota, Wisconsin and Michigan, bird hunting begins in late September and ends [for many hunters] in late October or early November."

When I initially read the report, thoughts of my favorite woodcock coverts began winging their way through my mind. My chest then began to tighten as I thought of the preponderance of tiny splashes of woodcock droppings dotting the alder leaves in all of my best haunts. Could this be a conspiracy? A favorite college hunting companion, with whom I regularly ditched class to go hunting, used to tell whatever lies it took to keep people away from *his* coverts. Could the blastomycosis bulletin be some deranged grouse hunter's scheme to keep hunters from entering the woods for the very same reason? Of course not, but the thought was just amusing enough for me to again relax my chest and think sensibly about the problem.

Before the advent of chemotherapy, the disease was fatal in more than 90 percent of cases! Today, a drug called amphotericin B has proven very effective in treating at least one form of the disease. Klein estimates that one in five people who contract the illness will die from it today. Research is continuing on additional drug treatments. For further information about blastomycosis, contact your physician or state department of health.

# The Best Place
# to Be a Grouse Hunter

*It has been written that Napolean's chest protruded a trifle more than nature intended, that the laurel wreath upon the brow of Julius Caesar fitted rather snugly at times, and that Alexander the Great had an inflated opinion of his own importance. Ah me? If only those historians could have seen that boy as he looked down on his first ruffed grouse.*

—Burton L. Spiller, *Drummer in the Woods*

# The Best Place
# to Be a Grouse Hunter

It is a lucky hunter who does not have to sit long behind the wheel of a car to get to grouse woods. Gary Wilson is one such hunter. He's a longtime friend whose house sits an aspen's length from grouse cover. Three sides of his setters' kennel are surrounded by blackberry—the living barbwire that grouse so dearly love.

His house blends comfortably with the Wisconsin woodland it inhabits. A romp with his setters through the woods awakes a napping ruff or perhaps a transient woodcock. Such are the pleasures of living in the heart of grouse country. I find myself fantasizing about one day homesteading in the midst of the best grouse-hunting region of North America, awakening to the sound of grouse drumming outside my bedroom window. A place where the birds always hold for a point and where neither blackberry, prickly ash, thistle, nor Lyme Disease thrive. Then, of course, I awaken.

Thanks to modern transport, though, I can be walking the grouse coverts with a pointer and side-by-side within hours of leaving the doldrums of the office. The ability to take people away from civilization is perhaps technology's greatest gift. But where is this mythical best grouse land? Pheasant hunters rave over South Dakota ringneck territory while quail hunters dream of a day on a Deep South plantation, but where does the grouse hunter find the partridge reigning as royalty?

I put that question to several of North America's leading grouse biologists and asked them to rank the ten best states and provinces in which to hunt ruffed grouse. Their answers were based on total grouse harvest, degree of access to good grouse habitat, numbers of hunters, grouse flushes per hunter hour, bag limit, and length of season. In all, seventeen states and provinces were named by the biologists on their lists of the top ten. By assigning a point value to each state and province using the frequency with and order in which it was given by each biologist, I was able to rank them statistically. Here, then, are the biologists' choices for best grouse hunting in North America:

| | |
|---|---|
| 1. Wisconsin | 6. Pennsylvania |
| 2. Minnesota | 7. New York |
| 3. Michigan | 8. Manitoba |
| 4. Ontario | 9. Washington |
| 5. Maine | 10. New Brunswick, Ohio, and Oregon (tied). |

The first three states—Wisconsin, Minnesota, and Michigan—were nearly interchangeable by most accounts. This coincides with the fact that these states are also the top money producers for the Ruffed Grouse Society. These states, according to the biologists, were easy selections to the top ten list. Enumerating states and provinces six through ten was not so clear-cut; a wide variety of rankings were given. Many felt that some western states could potentially offer superb ruffed grouse hunting, but little was known about hunting ruffs in the West.

The Great Lakes and New England states have a deeply rooted tradition, though, and the survey results favored those states. To the extent that harvest totals indicate the quality of a state or province's grouse hunting, the biologists—for the most part—concurred that the higher a state or province's harvest figures, the better the hunting. In 1988, Wisconsin Department of Natural Resources surveys concluded that 185,000 hunters took 653,000 grouse. It's important to keep in mind that harvest totals are actually more of an index by which to gauge rising and declining grouse numbers than they are an absolute tally of the number of birds taken.

From 1988 postcard surveys sent to Michigan hunters, state biologists were able to extrapolate that 160,000 hunters took nearly the same number of grouse as did Wisconsin hunters. Pat Corr, a biologist with the state of Maine, emphasized that his state's survey methods were very crude, but that in 1983, 116,000 hunters took roughly a half million grouse. New York biologist Jim Glidden said his figures suggest that 106,400 state hunters took roughly 330,000 grouse in 1988. Pennsylvania's 1988 harvest by its 390,000 grouse hunters was 523,000 birds.

Other statistics that support the biologists' rankings come from Ken Szabo, publisher of the bimonthly newsletter *Grouse Tales*, the official publication of the

To subscribe to *Grouse Tales*, send $9 to Ken Szabo, 17130 Chatfield, Cleveland, Ohio 44111. The subscription includes membership into the Loyal Order of Dedicated Grouse Hunters.

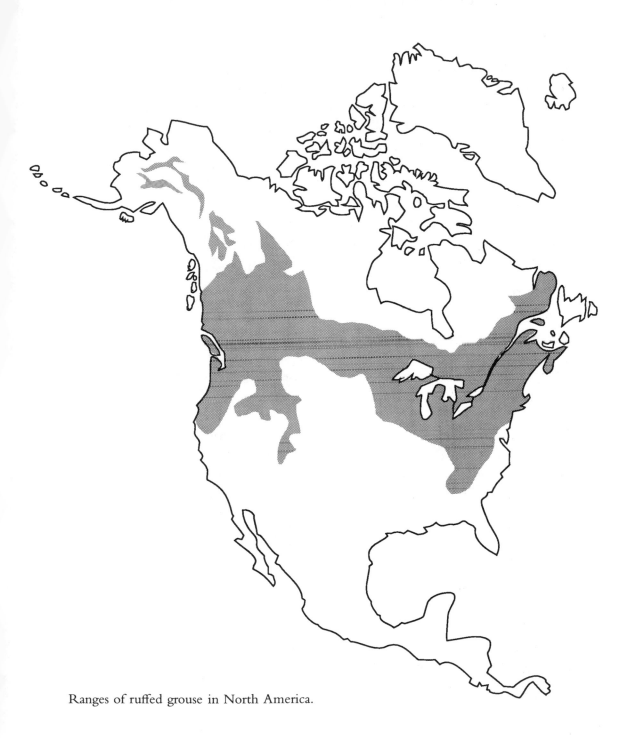

Ranges of ruffed grouse in North America.

Loyal Order of Dedicated Grouse Hunters. Szabo conducts an annual survey of his membership to determine hunter success by state. Here again, Wisconsin hunters reported the highest flush rate with an average of 3.25 grouse flushes per hour. One Badger State hunter, incidentally, reported taking 70 of 124 grouse shot at during the 1988–89 season. Other states with twenty or more responses to the survey included Michigan, with hunters reporting 2.58 flushes per hour; Pennsylvania, with 1.91 flushes; New York, with 1.61 flushes; West Virginia, with 1.51 flushes; and Ohio, with 1.46 flushes per hunter hour.

Should a trip to one of these favorite grouse-hunting locations be in your future, contact the appropriate state or provincial agency at the address listed below for further information.

Wisconsin Department of Natural
   Resources
Bureau of Wildlife Management
Box 7921
Madison, Wisconsin 53707 U.S.A.
Telephone 608/266-1877

Minnesota Department of Natural
   Resources
Division of Fish & Wildlife
Box 46, DNR Building
500 Lafayette Road
St. Paul, Minnesota 55155 U.S.A.
Telephone 612/296-6157

Michigan Department of Natural
   Resources
Wildlife Division
Box 30028
Lansing, Michigan 48909 U.S.A.
Telephone 517/373-1263

Ontario Ministry of Natural
   Resources
Public Information Center
Parliament Building
Toronto, Ontario M7A 1W3 Canada
Telephone 416/965-4251

Maine Department of Inland
   Fisheries & Wildlife
284 State Street
State House Station 41
Augusta, Maine 04333 U.S.A.
Telephone 207/289-2871

Pennsylvania Game Commission
2001 Elmerton Avenue
Harrisburg, Pennsylvania 17110-9797
   U.S.A.
Telephone 717/787-6286

New York Department of
  Environmental Conservation
Fish & Wildlife Division
50 Wolf Road
Albany, New York 12233 U.S.A.
Telephone 518/457-5400

Manitoba Department of Natural
  Resources
1495 St. James Street
Box 22
Winnipeg, Manitoba R3H 0W9
  Canada
Telephone 204/945-6784

Washington Department of Wildlife
600 Capitol Way North
Olympia, Washington 98504 U.S.A.
Telephone 206/753-5700

Oregon Department of Fish &
  Wildlife
506 Southwest Mill Street
Portland, Oregon 97207 U.S.A.
Telephone 503/229-5551

Ohio Department of Natural
  Resources
Division of Wildlife
1500 Dublin Road
Columbus, Ohio 43215 U.S.A.
Telephone 614/481-6345

New Brunswick Department of
  Natural Resources
Fish and Wildlife Branch
P.O. Box 6000
Fredericton, New Brunswick E3B
  5H1 Canada
Telephone 506/453-2433

Students at an Orvis Shooting School learn the fundamentals of instinctive wingshooting. This method of shooting is predicated on having a gun that properly fits the shooter and is on a proper gun mount. (*Photo © by Chris Dorsey*)

Drop at comb, drop at heel, length of pull, and pitch can all be determined by shooting a try gun at the range. Most factory-built guns are designed to fit an "average" shooter; people who don't fall into this category—short, tall, fat, or skinny shooters—may need a custom-built gun if they are to ever realize their true shooting potential. (*Photo © by Chris Dorsey*)

Gunsmith John Skinner adjusts a try gun used to develop a shooter's measurements, which become the basis for selecting or building a gun that fits properly. (*Photo © by Chris Dorsey*)

An Orvis shooting instructor (*left*) pays careful attention to all facets of a student's shooting technique. By recognizing faults early, the instructor is able to assist a student in making necessary corrections for better shooting results. (*Photo © by Chris Dorsey*)

Rick Rishell, director of the Orvis Shooting Schools, encourages artist Tim Joseph to concentrate on his target before mounting the gun. A shooter's eyes must be clearly focused on the target—not the bead of the shotgun—if the instinctive shooting method is to work. (*Photo © by Chris Dorsey*)

Wet woodlands provide the necessary growing conditions for the fungus responsible for blastomycosis. This infection is fatal in nearly 20 percent of the people infected. (*Photo © by Chris Dorsey*)

Sales of tick repellents have skyrocketed with the rapid spread of Lyme Disease. The Permanone line is one of the more effective brands on the market. (*Photo © by Chris Dorsey*)

This deer tick larva is resting next to a poppy seed. Detecting these tiny disease-carrying parasites is difficult, making the use of repellents all the more important. (*Photo © by Richard A. Bautz, University of Wisconsin*)

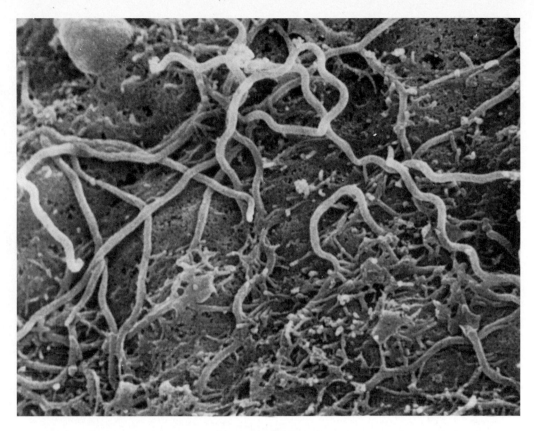

These corkscrew-shaped bacteria are Borrelia Burgdorferi, named for Dr. Willy Burgdorfer who discovered this spirochete responsible for Lyme Disease. These were taken from the Ixodes dammini, or deer tick, a common vector of Lyme in the Midwest and Northeast. (*Photo courtesy Willy Burgdorfer*)

The Rockies of Alberta provide a spectacular setting for some of the continent's finest grouse hunting. Ruffs in the West, however, receive little hunting pressure, and they are seldom as sophisticated as their eastern counterparts who are used to the sound of a shotgun blast. (*Photo © by George Cromwell*)

The forests of Manitoba are lightly hunted and offer some of North America's finest grouse hunting, as the author discovers here. (*Photo © by Chris Dorsey*)

These grouse will keep indefinitely in this Alberta hunting camp so long as temperatures remain below freezing. When thawed, the birds can be cleaned and soaked in cold saltwater until cooked or refrozen. (*Photo © by Chris Dorsey*)

A unique adaptation you have undoubtedly noticed while examining a grouse is the scalelike projections lining the edge of the grouse's toes. These pectinations give the bird's toes a centipede appearance, and it's believed that they allow the grouse to grip icy tree branches while feeding on buds during the winter months. (*Photo © by Chris Dorsey*)

Many hunters prefer to eviscerate grouse immediately after the kill in order to prevent any meat spoilage. The warmer the temperatures, of course, the faster decaying will progress. (*Photo* © *by Bob Robb*)

While many European recipes advocate aging or "mortifying" upland fowl, most Americans prefer their birds fresh. In either case, however, is there any better eating game bird? (*Photo © by David Kenyon*)

# From Field to Freezer

*The partridge that puffs to the shot string this morning at the edge of some frost-crisp apple orchard in the hills of Vermont is the selfsame bird—but totally different, of course—as the very first dove we ever knocked down, a lifetime ago, over a midwestern cornfield.*

—Robert F. Jones, "Everything Your Heart Desires"

# From Field to Freezer

About the time root cellars went out of vogue and farm boys grew up and moved to the city, the practice of hanging game birds to tenderize them was nearly lost. Ever so gradually, however, people are rediscovering the virtues of that past art much as they have the simple pleasures of gardening and splitting wood. Convenience, it seems, promises more than it often delivers.

Veteran farmers, still closely linked to their Old World roots, used to collect the chicken eggs in the morning before breakfast and take a stroll in the woods of the back forty to let their ham and eggs ruminate. They never carried over-and-unders, but were intimately familiar with the .22 resting inside the door of the milk house. Their quarry included squirrels, rabbits, and a grouse if they were lucky. Should their mission fail to harvest fur or fowl, an unsuspecting redwing was a suitable target to make certain the gun was still shooting straight.

While squirrels and rabbits were cleaned upon returning to the farmstead, grouse were simply hung from a string until ripe. The cool temperatures of the root cellar prevented the bird from spoiling quickly, while the bird's endemic bacteria began the slow decaying process. Today, the thought of eating anything that wasn't on ice within two hours of its death—whether chicken or rutabaga—is simply nauseating to most Americans. Aged birds, given the right conditions, commonly hung in the root cellar for a week or more before finally being plucked and prepared, thereby allowing human teeth and saliva to expedite the grouse's return to the soil.

Similarly, meat markets of yesteryear would hang a side of beef until it was nearly black from decay. Once properly aged, thick steaks would be cut from its loin and served in the upper-crust restaurants of the day. Though it sounds a bit barbaric for many, the effect was much the same as adding two coats of meat tenderizer before broiling. Imagine, if meat tenderizer quickly dissolves protein bonds, what must it do to those in the human stomach?

On the topic of meat tenderization, I was once asked what I do to prepare grouse in which I've hit hard. That was a surprisingly difficult question given that I could not recall ever centering a pattern on a grouse. "I compliment the person I'm hunting with," I answered.

## FIELD DRESSING GROUSE

Since most hunters simply take day trips to their favorite coverts, there's seldom an opportunity for grouse to spoil. If you happen to be hunting the early season when temperatures—even in the north woods—can reach the 70s and 80s, it's worthwhile to pause after you've taken a bird and eviscerate it by prying two fingers under the bird's breast and scooping out the entrails. Then put a handful of dry grass into the empty cavity of the bird to allow air to circulate and cool the meat. The leftover intestines won't last a day on the floor of a woods where nothing goes to waste.

One of the acquired skills of a great grouse hunter is the ability to know when to put down the shotgun and eviscerate a bird. It may seem a simple matter to some, but knowing when to perform this act is a valuable attribute. The inexperienced hunter will want to do it immediately. The experienced hunter knows, however, where one grouse flushes, often more wait. By setting down the gun in quality grouse cover, the hunter is tempting Providence, and a grouse will flush as certainly as ducks always fly the moment the coffee is being poured.

I often wait until my meanderings bring me to the edge of a clearing where I corral my setter to be certain he doesn't surprise any birds that might escape without a salute from my side-by-side. In moments, the process of disemboweling the bird is complete, and I once again continue my unending quest for grouse pockets.

## TO FREEZE OR NOT TO FREEZE?

When bird scent has evaporated for the day and my setter seems stuck in idle, I call him back and we stroll toward the pickup or camp. If camp is my destination, the birds will be placed in a cooler that has been tucked under a clump of sumac or similar shading bush. Well-insulated coolers do a remarkable job of storing cold night air for the duration of the sunlit hours. A sprinkling of salt over the meat is an added pinch of insurance that the meat won't spoil over a weekend or more. Liquid ice packs are a twentieth-century remedy to solving an Old World problem of meat spoilage. These packs last far longer than ice and never melt, creating a slurry at the bottom of the cooler as ice inevitably will. Upon returning home, I wash the grouse under cold running water and remove any BBs that might be lodged in the meat. It's easy to find the BBs by looking for the trail of what looks like a comet of feathers. I then soak the birds overnight in a solution of cold water and salt. The salt will draw any remaining blood from the meat and leave a more palatable morsel—though, in my opinion, even bad grouse is better than the best chicken.

Some hunters prefer to eat their birds in camp. I, on the other hand, have always shied from such practice. There are two reasons, really. First, I never, but never, jinx a grouse trip by assuming that I will shoot all the birds I need for dinner. Second, eating grouse is an event by itself. Long after the season has closed and the setters have heavy winter coats, I'll prepare a feast of roast grouse. As the cream sauce is poured over a trio of grouse breasts, my mind can once again wander to the steamy coverts of September or the crisp October morning in which I took the birds. Indeed, when you freeze your grouse, you enjoy the same hunt twice.

When I freeze fowl, I always write the date and location of the hunt on the outside of the freezer paper. I do this not because I fear the birds will go unused and suffer the most dastardly of deaths—freezer burn—rather it is a way to spark my hunting neurons into releasing the juices that allow my brain to think of grouse hunting.

With thoughts of bird days filling my mind and the aroma of grouse in cream sauce in my nostrils, I absorb the second half of the pleasure of grouse hunting. A bird as utterly and absolutely delectable as grouse would bring the price of lobster in the supergroceries across the land. But perhaps some of the flavor of grouse comes in knowing that most diners will never know what they are missing.

# Why We Kill for Grouse

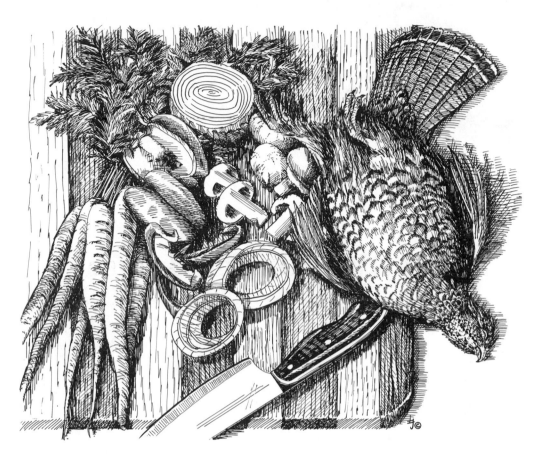

*Like lobster, mushrooms, escargot, trout, and other recognized delicacies, grouse should be savored more for its uniqueness than for its similarities to more common foods.*

—Dennis Walrod, *Grouse Hunter's Guide*

# Why We Kill For Grouse

The French have truffles. New Zealanders covet kiwi. But what would they give for the taste of grouse, ruffed grouse.

Had Noah a fancy for fowl, he'd have surely brought more than two ruffed grouse aboard the ark—perhaps making room by allowing the skunk, rattlesnake, scorpion, rat, flea, tick, and the like go adrift.

If it weren't for birds like the coot, however, we would never know the true heights to which the grouse has ascended on the gastronomic scale—it's the same way in which a diner can only truly appreciate beef Wellington after beef liver.

I was fourteen before I realized that pheasant wasn't the earth's finest dinner. I then entered a great period of personal enlightenment. My renaissance was brought on partly by tasting my first grouse and, to a lesser degree, by puberty.

Grouse are seldom served to large family gatherings or other assemblages of the probably unappreciative—no more than twenty-five-year-old Bordeaux would be offered them. Grouse—whether fried, broiled, roasted, fricasseed, or creamed— are shared only with those who understand and revel in the majesty of the entrée. Anyone can make you broiled lobster, but it is a very dear friend indeed who shares grouse with you.

I once saw a friend's daughter smother a grouse fillet in ketchup to "kill the gameness." Her otherwise reasonable father— a grouse hunter cum laude—stopped in midchew. He turned to his wife with a look of "Who raised this imp?"

If grouse were a beast easily attainable from the frozen foods section of a megamarket, its stock would fall considerably among those who enjoy each succulent bird proportionally to the amount of effort expended to shoot it. The grouse's resistance to domestication is a genuine sign of its nobility. While pheasant, quail, and even turkey have surrendered their avian spirit to life in a chicken coop, the grouse remains eternally wild. Perhaps it is for that reason that grouse serve as something of an inspiration to me as I work in a crowded high-rise above noisy, human-choked streets—a place in which I, like the chicken, while away my days in a cage where no contact with the land remains.

## MORTIFIED OR HORRIFIED?

Mortification, a practice of ageing game by letting the slow decay process begin, has its roots in central and western Europe. To most American hunters, a grouse that isn't cleaned, salted, and frozen within hours of having the life snuffed from it is a candidate for garden fertilizer. In fact, it isn't uncommon to read articles on the field care of game which steadfastly recommend that fowl be eviscerated immediately after the kill. The notion, of course, is that the sooner the meat is cooled the better. For my part, I have found no discernable difference in taste between the grouse cleaned immediately and its ripened counterpart that sometimes remains in my game vest for four or five hours.

Much of the European tradition, however, takes a radically different view of game care. In David Backus's book, *European Recipes for American Fish & Game*, he writes: "Traditionally, these 'ageings' are made on uneviscerated birds. The undamaged bird, supposedly does not putrefy, but decomposes from indigenous organisms. Brillat Savarin, perhaps the greatest of French culinary artists in international reputation, commended hanging 'le faisan' until the abdomen turned green! Grimond de la Reyniere said a pheasant killed at Mardi Gras would be ready to prepare on Easter!"

The key words from this paragraph by Backus are "undamaged bird." It is a talented hunter who can scare prey to death. In actuality, though, Backus is referring to a bird that has sustained little damage from the mortal shot. When the skin is broken and large BBs driven through a bird's carcass, foreign organisms are allowed to enter the bird, ruining its potential to be aged. Conversely, a bird that has sustained little damage will age properly because the only microbes involved in the decomposition process are those already native to the bird's body.

Fowl can be hung for as little as a few days to over a week depending on temperature. The cooler the temperature, the slower the ageing process. A range of 45 to 55 degrees Fahrenheit might be considered optimal for ageing. Many Europeans fervently argue that only aged game, like rested wine, will reach its full culinary potential.

Backus continues that "hung game is almost invariably marinated before cooking. Use your recipes for un-marinated birds on fresh game; the more exotic marinated formulas are at their best with well hung birds. Red wine marinades are in order: white wine marinades are best reserved for fresh meat. . . . Use great care cleaning birds for the marinade, progress by easy stages to longer hangings. Above all, never fool yourself on the intact character of your birds. Spoiled meat is dangerous to eat, and gives game a bad name among the uninitiated. Both are to studiously avoid!"

## RECIPES

Here, then, is an assortment of recipes for grouse—both fresh and aged—that will introduce you to the second half of an enjoyable grouse hunt.

## MANDARIN GROUSE

Season three grouse with salt and pepper; place a single orange slice in the cavity of each bird. Wrap each grouse in bacon slices and roast in 350 degree oven for 25 minutes. Baste the birds frequently with a citrus mixture.

To make the citrus mixture for three grouse, combine and simmer for two minutes:

shredded orange peel
1 teaspoon lemon juice
1 tablespoon orange juice concentrate
4 cups butter or margarine
2 tablespoons water.

When the birds are cooked, remove the bacon and orange slices. Serve garnished with glazed orange slices and parsley. Allow one grouse per person.

## DREAM GROUSE

3 grouse, jointed, seasoned with salt and pepper
1 can cream of mushroom soup
¼ cup water
¼ cup dry white wine
1 6-ounce can sliced mushrooms, drained

Put the birds in a crock pot. Mix the soup, water, and wine and pour over the grouse; add the mushrooms. Cover and cook on low heat for seven to eight hours. Serves three.

## SCOTTISH-STYLE GROUSE

1 plucked grouse
½ cup bread crumbs
3 tablespoons butter
2 raw chicken livers, mashed
1 teaspoon parsley
onion juice

allspice
pork lard
1 scant cup chicken broth
black truffles or morel mushrooms
white wine

Fill the cavity of the grouse with a mixture of ½ cup bread crumbs, profusely buttered, and an equal part of raw mashed chicken livers, 1 teaspoon parsley, a few drops onion juice, and a pinch of allspice.

Blanket the grouse with a thin slice of pork lard. Truss and place in a braising kettle, the bottom of which contains a scant cup of chicken broth. Arrange on top four thin slices of black truffles or morel mushrooms. Adjust the cover hermetically and braise the birds for 25 minutes at 450 degrees. Remove from the oven, dress the bird on a hot platter, and surround with fresh large mushrooms peeled and sautéed in butter.

Place the kettle in which the bird was cooked over a hot fire until the liquid is reduced to nearly nothing, then add a wine glass of white wine. Boil for two or three minutes, strain through a fine sieve, and pour over bird. Present with red currant jelly and applesauce. Serves one splendidly.

## SIMPLY GROUSE

6 skinned or plucked grouse
2 tablespoons flour
½ cup butter, melted
1 cup orange juice
¼ teaspoon salt per bird
⅛ teaspoon pepper per bird
½ cup sherry

Place the grouse in large roasting bag with the other ingredients. Shake the contents well; roast one hour at 300 degrees.

Pour the drippings over birds and accompany with cranberries and wild rice. Serves six.

## BAKED GROUSE WITH PECAN STUFFING

4 grouse
¼ cup butter, melted
¼ cup pecan nuts, coarsely chopped
1 cup dry bread cubes
2 tablespoons flour
1½ teaspoon salt
½ cup butter
¼ cup sherry
2 chicken bouillon cubes dissolved in 1½ cups hot water

In a medium-sized frying pan, melt ¼ cup butter over low heat; stir in the pecan meats and brown slightly—do not burn. Stir in the bread cubes; toss lightly. Stuff birds with the mixture. Close each cavity with a small skewer and place the birds in a casserole dish. Combine salt and flour, sprinkle over the birds, and drip with ½ cup melted butter. Bake birds for 12 minutes at 450 degrees.

In a small saucepan, combine sherry and bouillon and pour over the grouse. Cover, decrease the oven temperature to 350 degrees, and bake 50 minutes. Uncover and bake an additional 50 minutes or until the birds are golden brown. Serves four.

## CREAMY GROUSE

3 grouse, jointed
¼ cup butter
1 chicken bouillon cube dissolved in ½ cup hot water
2 tablespoons red currant jelly
1 cup cream
1 tablespoon brandy
chopped parsley
fresh asparagus

Fry the jointed grouse with butter in a large skillet until brown; place birds in a casserole dish. Add the bouillon, cover, and bake in the oven for roughly 40 minutes at 425 degrees. Remove the grouse to a platter and keep warm.

Reduce bouillon and drippings by half. Stir in red currant jelly, then the cream. Flame the brandy, then add to the sauce. Pour sauce over birds; garnish with chopped parsley and fresh asparagus. Serves three.

## PAPRIKA GROUSE

2 grouse
2 cups onions, finely chopped
¼ cup butter
2 tablespoons tomato puree
2 teaspoons sugar
4 tablespoons paprika
3 tablespoons flour
1 cup grouse (or chicken) stock, heated
1 cup red wine
1 cup sour cream
2 tablespoons chopped parsley

Brown the grouse and onions with butter in a large skillet; place in a casserole dish. In a separate bowl, blend the tomato puree, sugar, paprika, and flour. Stir in two tablespoons of hot stock. Add this mixture, the wine, and remaining stock to casserole. Add desired seasoning, cover, and bake for 55 minutes at 350 degrees. Remove the grouse to a platter; cover and keep warm.

Stir a little of the sauce into the sour cream to prevent curdling; add the sour cream to the sauce in the casserole. Blend thoroughly and pour over the grouse. Garnish lightly with chopped parsley. Serves two.

## GROUSE DEVON

2½ cups cubed cooked grouse (pressure-cook until well-done)
2 10-ounce packages frozen broccoli spears, steamed until tender
½ cup real mayonnaise
2 cans cream of chicken soup
1 can cream of mushroom soup
1 teaspoon lemon juice
½ cup grated cheddar cheese
½ cup crushed corn flakes

Place the steamed broccoli in a shallow casserole. Arrange the grouse over the broccoli. Combine the mayonnaise, soups, and lemon juice and heat until liquid. Pour over the grouse and broccoli; sprinkle with cheese. Bake for 20 minutes at 350 degrees.

Uncover, add the crushed corn flakes, and bake for an additional 10 minutes. Serves five.

# References

Allen, Durward. *Our Wildlife Legacy*. Funk & Wagnalls Company, New York, NY, 1954.

Anderson, Tom. *Learning Nature by a Country Road*. Voyageur Press, Stillwater, MN, 1989.

Atwater, Sally, and Judith Schnell, eds. *Ruffed Grouse*. Stackpole Books, Harrisburg, PA, 1989.

Bodio, Stephen. *Good Guns*. Nick Lyons Books, New York, NY, 1986.

Boughton, D. C., and J. J. Volk. "Avian Hosts of Eimerian Coccidia." *Bird Banding* 9 (1938): 140-150.

Bowlen, Bruce. *The Orvis Wing-Shooting Handbook*. Nick Lyons Books, New York, NY, 1985.

Bump, G., R. W. Darrow, F. C. Edminster, and W. F. Crissey. *The Ruffed Grouse: Life History, Propagation, Management*. 1947. Reprint. New York State Conservation Department, Albany, NY, 1978.

Carty, David. "Grouse Of A Different Color." *Shooting Sportsman*, April/May 1989, 34–37.

Davis, Henry P. *Training Your Own Bird Dog*. G. P. Putnam's Sons, New York, NY, 1969.

Duffey, David Michael. *Bird Hunting Tactics*. Willow Creek Press, Wautoma, WI, 1978.

Evans, George. "The Thorns." *Shooting Sportsman*, October/November 1988, 4–8.

Gregg, Larry. *Population Ecology of Woodcock In Wisconsin*. Technical Bulletin No. 144, Wisconsin Department of Natural Resources, 1984.

Gullion, Gordon. *Ruffed Grouse Research at the University of Minnesota Cloquet Forestry Center*. Minnesota Department of Natural Resources Wildlife Research Unit 1985 Report, 1986.

Jones, Robert F. "Everything Your Heart Desires." From *Seasons of the Hunter*. Alfred A. Knopf, New York, NY, 1985.

Kubisiak, John F. *Ruffed Grouse Habitat Relationships in Aspen and Oak Forests of Central Wisconsin*. Technical Bulletin No. 151, Wisconsin Department of Natural Resources, 1981.

Leopold, Aldo. *A Sand County Almanac*. Ballentine Books, New York, NY, 1966.

Rau, Ron. *Sage Lake Road*. Willow Creek Press, Wautoma, WI, 1983.

Reynolds, Mike. *Shooting Made Easy*. The Crowood Press, Ramsbury, Wiltshire, England, 1986.

Robinson, William L. *Ruffed Grouse Management: State of the Art in the Early 1980s*. Wildlife Society and Ruffed Grouse Society, St. Louis, MO, 1983.

Sisley, Nick. *Grouse and Woodcock: An Upland Hunter's Book*. Stackpole Books, Harrisburg, PA, 1980.

Smith, A. J. *Sporting Clays*. Willow Creek Press, Wautoma, WI, 1989.

Smith, Steve. *Hunting Upland Game Birds*. Stackpole Books, Harrisburg, PA, 1987.

Spiller, Burton L. *Grouse Feathers*. Derrydale Press, Lyon, MS, 1935.

Thompson, Donald, and John Moulton. *An Evaluation of Wisconsin Ruffed Grouse Surveys*. Wisconsin Department of Natural Resources, 1981.

Walrod, Dennis. *Grouse Hunter's Guide*. Stackpole Books, Harrisburg, PA, 1985.

Woolner, Frank. *Timberdoodle!* Nick Lyons Books, New York, NY, 1974.

Woolner, Frank. *Grouse and Grouse Hunting*. Nick Lyons Books, New York, NY, 1970.

# Index